PRAISE FOR
GET ROOTED

"Robyn Moreno truly reclaims and educates us on our ancestors' contributions to traditional medicine and suggestions of remembering our ancestors' holistic healing of mind, body, and spirit."

—Dr. Eliseo Torres, professor of Curanderismo at the University of New Mexico and author of *Curanderismo: The Art of Traditional Medicine without Borders* and *Curandero: A Life in Mexican Folk Healing*

"Robyn brilliantly reclaims our ancestral medicines and shares her inspirational journey of how they helped her to reclaim herself. Her willingness to be raw and vulnerable is soul medicine that is shared with the reader. The guided meditations and limpia rites are also a beautiful way to decompress and journey into our own healing work. I absolutely love this book!"

—Erika Buenaflor, MA, JD, author of *Cleansing Rites of Curanderismo* and *Veneration Rites of Curanderismo*

"I love this book. I love the question that Robyn Moreno asked and answered in her own life: Am I acting from *susto* or *ser*—from a loss of soul, or from my essence, my truth? And I love how she uses stories from her own life, and from the richness of her lineage, and from the methods of Curanderismo—the medicine of her Mexican grandmothers—to give us a roadmap to ask and answer that essential question for ourselves."

—Elizabeth Lesser, cofounder Omega Institute, *New York Times* author of best-selling books including *Broken Open: How Difficult Times Can Help Us Grow* and *Cassandra Speaks: When Women Are the Storytellers the Human Story Changes*

"This book is a gift from *las abuelas*. A modern yet ancient book that carries wisdom to last generations to come. If you are looking for a soul-nourishing read, this is it!"

—Christine Gutierrez, best-selling author of
*I Am Diosa: A Journey to Healing Deep, Loving
Yourself, and Coming Back Home to Soul*

"A beautiful read, rich with intimate stories that will inspire you to reclaim your roots and discover your magic."

—Sheleana Aiyana, founder of Rising Woman,
and author of *Becoming the One*

"Sometimes we have to go backward in order to leap forward. This book is a powerful guide of remembrance, reclamation, and renewal. Robyn's story of healing through accessing the medicine of her lineage reminds us all that the truest healing isn't something we're separate from. It's as close as our own DNA, our own breath, and the people we inherited it all from."

—Kate Northrup, best-selling author of *Do Less:
A Revolutionary Approach to Time and
Energy Management for Ambitious Women*

GET
ROOTED

GET
ROOTED

Reclaim Your Soul, Serenity, and
Sisterhood Through the Healing Medicine
of the Grandmothers

ROBYN MORENO

hachette
BOOKS

NEW YORK

Note: The information in this book is true and complete to the best of our knowledge. This book is intended only as an informative guide for those wishing to know more about health issues. In no way is this book intended to replace, countermand, or conflict with the advice given to you by your own physician. The ultimate decision concerning care should be made between you and your doctor. We strongly recommend you follow their advice. Information in this book is general and is offered with no guarantees on the part of the authors or Hachette Go. The authors and publisher disclaim all liability in connection with the use of this book.

Hachette Go, an imprint of Hachette Books
Hachette Book Group
1290 Avenue of the Americas
New York, NY 10104
HachetteGo.com
Facebook.com/HachetteGo
Instagram.com/HachetteGo

First Edition: June 2023

Hachette Books is a division of Hachette Book Group, Inc.
The Hachette Go and Hachette Books name and logos are trademarks of Hachette Book Group, Inc.

Hachette Go books may be purchased in bulk for business, educational, or promotional use. For information, please contact your local bookseller or Hachette Book Group Special Markets Department at special.markets@hbgusa.com.

The publisher is not responsible for websites (or their content) that are not owned by the publisher.

Library of Congress Cataloging-in-Publication Data has been applied for.

ISBNs: 9780306926273 (hardcover); 9780306926280 (ebook)

Printed in the United States of America

LSC-C

Printing 2, 2023

To my parents, whose roots grew me
To my husband and daughters, whose love roots me

Contents

Author's Note

Some names and details have been changed out of consideration for friends and loved ones. Sacred practices have been shared with permission from my *maestrxs* and ancestors. *Curanderismo* means "a way of healing" in Spanish and broadly describes the varied healing practices used throughout Latin America. In this book, when I refer to Curanderismo, I am referring to the traditional medicine of Mexico because as a Mexican American from the Southwest, that is the tradition I grew up with and practice, though the medicine does vary and evolve with each practitioner.

While this book shares teachings from Curanderismo, it does not initiate you as a *curandera/o/x*. If you're interested in the beautiful medicine of Curanderismo, take the time to study with a knowledgeable teacher. More than anything, this is a book about spiritual reclamation, and I hope it inspires you to rediscover, learn about, and practice medicine from your own sacred lineage.

GET
ROOTED

Introduction

Tlaalahui, tlapetzcahui in tlalticpac (It is slippery, it is slick on the earth).

—*Mexica proverb*

"You're so rooted!" gushed Roma, a bubbly energy healer—and hairstylist—from Seattle. Her business card promised, "Healing from Hair to Heart!"

"Yeah, you're the only one here who's actually *in* your body," echoed her sister, Antonette, a laid-back wildlife biologist/curandera who was leading our retreat in Belize.

Our group had just finished an intense meditation where we journeyed down into a cave (real) to ride a jaguar (imagined) to help us break through mental and spiritual blocks. I was feeling a lot of emotions after flying on my fictitious jaguar, but grounded wasn't topping the charts. So when these spiritual sisters zeroed in on my rootedness, I stopped and looked at them curiously—because for most of my life, I have felt really unanchored.

As a Gemini, I have a natural airiness that I like to think of as easygoing but that can present as dreamy or forgetful. Because busy can be my default mode, I've been called a *tormenta* and a spinning top, since I was always whirling and moving. But if we are really going to get into it—which is why we're here, right?—the truth is, I've also had my fair share of life trauma, which had unleashed a wrecking ball right through my emotional foundation.

So to say I was working on becoming rooted was an understatement. I had been healing, purging, praying, rooting, and retrieving for the past 240 days as if my life depended on it—because, well, it had. Just one year before arriving in this remote farm in western Belize with these soulful siblings and a circle of curanderas, I'd had a full-on midlife meltdown.

For the most part, it was that familiar working-mom tightrope walk of trying to do it all that so many parents around the world face. Most of the rom-com elements were there:

- The charmingly scattered mom who runs maniacally to catch the commuter train after dropping off her adorable kids at day care
- The dependable hubby who's starting to lose his stoic cool after one too many nights waiting for #momboss to come home from yet another late work dinner
- Climactic work scenes (Deadlines! Firings! Bad press! High-stakes deals!)
- The relatable sense that no matter what our scrappy heroine does, she is still—spectacularly—failing at everything

But the circumstances, the pressure, and the consequences made it all feel deeper—and darker—than the usual *Bad Moms* comedy. Like that memorable time I hid in the bathroom during our work Christmas party so I could watch my older daughter's preschool holiday recital via FaceTime. I had chosen work over family—again—so there I sat on the toilet, watching Lucia sweetly sing "Let It Snow," feeling guilty as I gulped a glass of white wine that I was balancing on the toilet paper dispenser, wondering what I was doing with my life.

So many signs and so many slips, and yet I kept running forcefully right through them all—until that night I ended up on the floor.

I had been organizing an important leadership conference for the media company I worked for, and because budgets were limited, we all took on an overwhelming amount of extra work, with me acting as producer, host, and emcee all at once. Our small but mighty team busted our asses, and the event was a rousing success. We had somehow pulled it off—again. High on a stage in front of a crowd of three hundred people, I closed the conference by giving an inspiring speech.

After I got off the stage and took a train ride back to my riverfront town in the Hudson Valley of New York, I met up with a group of friends at a beautiful waterside restaurant to celebrate and decompress with many crisp bottles of Sancerre. It was a festive and well-deserved revelry, and after holding it together for everyone else, all I wanted was to drink myself silly and just fall apart.

Which is just what I did five hours and three bars later, when I drunkenly fell off my stool trying to take a group selfie and smashed my nose on a table. I blurrily remember people looking down at me: friends, my husband, and even my daughters, because somewhere in the merriment, I had convinced my husband, Lars, and our kids to join me.

Recognizing that *that* was the end of the party, we quickly left and went home, and I faintly remember sloppily hugging the girls good night before I staggered to our bed and passed out.

The next morning, I woke up with a pounding headache and crusted blood on the front of the beautiful boho dress I was still wearing from the day before. It wasn't even my dress; I had borrowed it for the event. Panicked, I ran to the bathroom and gasped when I looked in the mirror and saw a jagged gash on my nose and fear in my eyes staring back at me. "It's okay, it's okay, it's okay," I kept saying to myself like a mantra to calm the rising horror in my chest as I reached into the cabinet to grab some aspirin. "It's okay, it's okay, it's okay," I repeated as I gingerly lifted my dress over my head, careful to avoid my injured face. "It's okay, it's okay, it's okay," I chanted as I turned on the faucet to run the stained fabric under cold water. But as I watched rusty blood seep out of my dress and spiral in slow motion down the drain, I had a thought as firm as the bathroom sink I was gripping: "I am not okay."

The Mexica* called the world "slippery slick."

They believed the world was an unstable place, a place where you could trip and fall, either from your poor judgments or from the inherent slipperiness of life. In the *Florentine Codex*, an account of Mexica life compiled by the Franciscan missionary Bernardino de Sahagún, a mother warns her daughter, "The earth is not a place of contentment . . . it is a place of joy with fatigue, of joy with pain."

This concept might be new to you, but I'll bet it feels familiar. We are happily walking along in our lives when—*bam!*—curve balls come from every corner. We lose our jobs, loved ones betray us, and we surprise ourselves with our weaknesses, our ugly anger, our scary ability to hurt and be hurt. We've all experienced the world's slickness in our own different ways: it's our friend who senselessly cheats on her loving husband, the neighbor who's abusing Adderall to keep up with her busy life, or the cousin who's overdrawn her account because of the shopping addiction she just can't seem to quit.

Slippery slick is that "Fuck! Here we go again"–ness that heaves you over the edge of a cliff, propelled by your own internal pain, broken promises, or other outside forces, like, say, a global pandemic that strikes out of nowhere and drop-kicks all of our perfectly laid-out and sweat-drenched dreams right into the dirt.

Yup, the world is slippery, all right. Yet as gruesome as that bathroom moment was for me, when fear and shame kept pummeling me in waves, I grasped on to something rooted deep within me.

I didn't know what it was called then. I just felt its pulsing, hopeful signal sent from somewhere ancient and far below that whispered there could be another way: another way to work, another way to mother, another way to walk on this slippery slick path.

So, clinging on to that life raft of a possibility, I began to *Get Rooted*.

---

* *Aztec* is a word given by scholars to refer to the rulers of ancient central Mexico, who spoke Nahuatl. But the "Aztecs" never called themselves *Aztecs*, instead referring to themselves as the Mexica.

I have always been a spiritual seeker, lighting candles to La Virgen de Guadalupe while simultaneously studying Eastern religions and philosophies. In my thirties, I became a yoga teacher and life coach. My shelves are lined with self-help books with wisdom from people I love and admire—from Michelle Obama to Dr. Clarissa Pinkola Estés. But something in that bathroom moment screamed out an urgent SOS, and, mercifully, something closer to home answered back.

In that Cosmic Big Brother way that you might just think, "My kid is growing out of her shorts," and suddenly ads for Target start popping up *everywhere*, I started to see messages all centered around Curanderismo—an earth-based healing tradition that blends the beliefs, medicine, and practices of Indigenous peoples of the Americas, Africa, and Europe—and their respective histories—and utilizes energetic cleansings, herbs, heart-to-heart talks, touch, sound healing, prayer, and more to help balance your emotions, spirit, and body.

A year prior, my cousin Patty, who was studying to be a curandera, asked one of her instructors to come to New York City to teach a small group of people, including me, the art and wisdom of Curanderismo. Even though I was dizzy with the stresses of work and family, something unclenched in me during the session. I had felt at home with the teachings and the tools because my great-grandmother had been a practicing curandera.

Now I began to feel that call coming from deep inside. "Can I heal whatever is going on with me and my family by learning the medicine of my grandmothers?" I wondered.

And with that guiding question in mind, I set out.

Eventually I resigned from my job, switching back to a freelance career that was more freeing but less financially steady. I knew it was a precarious, and privileged, decision to walk away from that manic #momboss life, but I did it.

I began to study Curanderismo with a sixty-five-year-old *chingona*—badass—reverend. Among the many life-changing things she taught me was the concept of Ser: your true essence, the whole and unbreakable you.

I wish someone would have told me how much I'd have to fall apart before I found my wholeness.

"What did you expect, *comadre*?" she replied when I complained about how painfully hard this all was.

What *did* I expect when I started on this spiritual journey?

A movie version of healing, maybe, where I would magically solve my midlife breakdown and never-ending family drama in a clever, madcap, and perfectly wrapped-up ninety-minute bow? Instead, it would turn out to be a 260-day long journey that twisted and turned and took me backward, inward, and down, down, down to the root of it all.

I wished someone had told me that once you start opening the doors and windows of memories and secrets that the winds will blow. They'll rip your house right off its foundation and rattle and roar through every part of you.

I wish someone had told me about all the revelations, abominations, and transformations to come: the blessed and wretched discoveries, the agonizing peeling off of skins, the exhausted miracle of rebirth, and the restoring joy of finally coming home.

I wish someone had told me as I set out on this journey that I thought I had so ingeniously crafted (but was probably ancestrally arranged) that I'd gain so much but also lose so much.

I wish someone had told me.

But would I have listened?

In the distance, I saw a light shining like a beacon, and I ran for it.

I didn't know it was a fire.

When I emerged from my journey nearly nine months later, staring down my forty-sixth birthday—the age my father was when he died—I had changed. Truths had been revealed, my Ser and self-trust reclaimed.

I was rooted.

And now, as a storyteller and practitioner of Curanderismo, I help myself and others get—and stay—rooted because healing isn't a destination so much as a lifelong remembering, where we release, reclaim, and root back—again and again.

And getting rooted is not a journey we walk alone. I believe in collective healing because I have been healed and cradled and nurtured back to root by my circle. The group of people who saw me flat on that floor are the same ones who extended their hands to pick me up. It is in circle, in community, and in connection that we root. Those are the ways of the ancestors. Those are the ways we need now.

Getting rooted means living the life you're meant to live while letting go of who you think you should be. Getting rooted means making your own map instead of following the one that society gave you. Getting rooted means finding your way home to that holy place of peace where you can receive, and retrieve, your gifts because you got rooted into trusting yourself and the quiet knowing of your body.

If you're struggling, like so many of us are, repeating the same patterns, feeling painfully anxious, woefully stuck, and finding that the same well-worn ways we try to handle our lives just aren't working anymore, then I share my own story here in the hopes that you might see a sliver of yourself reflected back in these pages and know that you are not alone. My 260-day healing journey is broken up into five parts—the east, north, west, south, and center—because I was guided by each direction to find my way home. I also offer you some of the tools I've collected in my medicine bag to help you feel lifted and steadied until you find yourself rooted and ready to walk again on this all-too-short, slippery slick thing we call life.

The book you hold in your hands is my *ofrenda* to you. It is an invitation to call your power back. It's a beacon to find your way home. And it's a reminder to get rooted and reclaim what has always been yours.

Your Ser.

PART ONE

The East:
Here's to Your New Beginning

1

Finding Your Way

I arrived in Mexico spent and sun deprived after quitting my job only a few weeks earlier. Something had changed in me after the "bathroom incident." That low, emotionally hungover feeling I'd had that day stayed with me the next day and the next—and for the first time in my life, I couldn't seem to snap myself out of it. Ever since that frightening moment when I saw my own blood circling down my bathroom sink, I kept asking myself, "What are you bleeding for?"

The truth was, I had been wounded for a while. Or at least since my dad died of pancreatic cancer when I was just thirteen. One summer he was swimming with me and my three sisters in the Guadalupe River under the blazing Texas sun, and the next summer he was gone—slipping away and under, as we watched helplessly—taking with him our family's stability, our wholeness, and his wisdom of how this slippery slick world worked.

My father was our gravity, and without him, my mom, my three sisters, and I all flew apart. My mom, who was widowed at just forty with four daughters and two businesses to take care of, drowned her grief by working constantly, getting a new boyfriend, and picking up a chain-smoking habit. I was charged with taking care of my two little sisters, while my older sister helped out by running my dad's ballroom. It was a caretaking role that became threaded into my identity.

I was the pretty classic people-pleasing middle kid. I was the easy baby, the smiling sister. This likable persona became cemented after my dad died because as my three sisters acted out for the attention and love they needed by rebelling and even running away, I just didn't dare bring my mom any more grief. Things in our blown-apart family became even more unstable when we moved into a brand-new home our father designed for us on his deathbed. It was a dying present for my mom, who always wanted a bigger house than the one-story, one-bathroom one we grew up in, but the change of schools and culture further added to our instability.

At my new richer, and whiter, school, I was lost—a nobody in an endless sea of blond and wealth. Luckily, I found my way when a history teacher recruited me for the debate team. I loved politics and current events, something I inherited from my father, who was a government major and into the Chicano movement of the 1960s and 1970s. I especially liked our assistant coach, who was encouraging and who quietly covered my costs for competing in out-of-town tournaments when I told her I couldn't afford to go.

After high school, I attended the University of Texas at Austin, where I missed my dad's counsel and support more than ever. He'd been the one who helped me craft my campaign speech when I ran for student council. He nurtured my intelligence and enrolled us both in after-school computer courses, where we had precious time together to chat and eat dill pickles and *chamoy*. I yearned for my father so much in those college years and hated that I couldn't share all that I was learning in Mexican American history or ask advice on whether to major in broadcast journalism or political science. But I found a way to manage my pain. Austin was a party college town, and here my drinking caught fire.

Unsurprisingly, I dropped out after two years with failing grades and three majors. I had learned how to survive but not how to sustain. A guidance counselor told me I needed to be inspired and encouraged me to use my time away from school to travel. I spent a few meandering years working as a hotel concierge, cocktail waitressing in Las Vegas, experimenting with a lot of drugs, and basically being a nineties slacker. I finally found my motivation to go back to school one day after I had to wait on a table of rich girls I had gone to high school with. We chatted as I took their drink order, and they told me how they had graduated from not only college but also law school and were all engaged. I stood there in my waiter's uniform, smiling back and fake laughing. But instead of delivering the drinks they ordered, I took off my apron, told my manager I had to leave immediately, and walked out the door. When I got in my car, I turned on the ignition, blasted the radio, and drove straight to UT Austin to enroll in the upcoming fall semester. I felt my dad with me that day. I knew in my heart I was ready for my next level.

I graduated from university with a degree in communications the following year and was in my college bookstore trying to figure out jobs when my eyes locked on something mesmerizing: a beautiful brown-skinned Latina on the cover of a magazine. I loved women's fashion magazines, but I rarely saw women with anything close to my ethnic background on their covers or in their pages. Flipping through the glossy pages, I saw stories that celebrated my culture in ways I had never, ever seen in the media growing up: a magazine written by Latinas for Latinas. I began to dream a new dream. I knew immediately that this was where I would work.

I bought a one-way ticket from Austin to New York City, crashed with my little sister Paloma, who had just moved there to go to school for fashion design, wrote my résumé, and hand delivered it to the magazine's offices. I was shaking with excitement as I walked into a gigantic high-rise building in the heart of Times Square and up to their glass door.

A girl walked out and almost ran me over as I stood clutching my résumé. "Can I help you?" she asked.

"I want a job!" I blurted out.

Not sure what to do with this eager stranger on the doorstep, she summoned another woman, who again asked, "Can I help you?"

Turned out they needed a fact-checker, and less than an hour after walking into the offices, I was offered the position.

Even after years of working my way up the ranks in the media industry, that day still stands as one of the best experiences of my life.

It meant that much more when I landed back at that magazine almost twenty years later—but this time as editor in chief.

To me, we were never just a magazine or a media company—we were on a mission to show the world the talent, ingenuity, and diversity we knew existed within our community.

Although running the magazine was my dream job, it was slowly killing me because things had changed drastically in the publishing landscape. Print media was already in free fall, with beloved magazines closing left and right. But as a small, independent company, we felt the changes faster and deeper. Layoffs began to happen on the regular, with even loyal, long-term employees being let go. Yet I had run into that burning building thinking, "We can save this!"

Hard work and enduring optimism have always been my signature traits—in many ways, my survival skills. So along with our talented team, we doubled down: redefining our mission, growing our e-commerce site, and launching our first-ever digital issues.

After three grueling years at the magazine, I was proud of what we had achieved, but it came at a cost. I was working long hours, seven days a week, and my hectic work and travel schedule kept me away from my young family. Even when I was home, I wasn't "there"; instead, I was constantly checking emails, scanning headlines for breaking news, or just obsessing. While we had made amazing strides, we were still in such financial jeopardy that the New York Post reported on our travails, including paying our staff and freelancers late. I felt the walls closing in on us.

Back at home, my three sisters and our mother were suffering through their own near collapses—some far more dire. Lety, the oldest, was in the early stages of recovery after years of substance use. Apolonia, my younger sister, was enduring the challenges of single motherhood. Paloma, my baby sister, had her shit together career-wise but still felt lost in her personal life. And after too many years of struggle, my mother still couldn't seem to catch the break she deserved and was still working and stressing at an age when she should have been retiring.

I had always been a fast-moving free spirit, but I had begun to question why I was moving so fast and whether my spirit was free—or just fleeing.

With this job, I'd become someone I didn't recognize, someone who chose work over her family and well-being again and again. I used to be a yoga teacher, but health was last on my list as a #boss-bitch. Lars used to ask me, not ironically, "What happened to the Robyn I married?" when he saw me staying up late working, downing glasses of cabernet and chunks of parmesan for dinner. The stress and exhaustion got so bad that I developed vertigo and was once whisked away from my office in an ambulance because the world was spinning so much, I had crouched beneath my desk and couldn't get up. The world was slippery slick, and I literally couldn't find my footing.

Not long after the bar incident, I finally decided to resign.

Thawing in my backyard under the shining sun, I watched my kids play but also habitually kept checking my multiple email accounts and phones. For days, I had scores of emails and texts: "Congrats!" "Best of luck!" "Guuurl! What happened?" "Want to meet?" "What's next for you?"

What's *next* for me? I had no idea. Without my job, I felt utterly and completely lost.

Then my cousin Flo invited me to her thatch-roofed *palapa* in the village of Puerto Morelos, outside of Cancun, Mexico, to help celebrate her birthday. Less than an hour after arriving at Flo's home—a jungle oasis with climbing vines in the courtyard and hanging hammocks—I ran two blocks and immersed my weary body in the gloriously warm waters of the Caribbean Sea, and it felt like a cleansing. When my cousins Flo and Patty and my eighty-two-year-old *tía*, Ximena, came to find me on the beach, calling my name, I was so relaxed, I thought I was dreaming for a moment.

We went out for *tacos de pescado* at an outdoor restaurant over-looking the ocean. Walking home, arms linked with my family through the town square and under the stars, their gentle touch and closeness triggered a thought that ran through my mind and body: "Maybe it's time to stop running."

I breathed in that salty air, and it occurred to me that my long-worn tendency to achieve and be helpful may not be as selfless as I thought. That maybe my *over*functioning, *over*stressing, running in circles trying to save everything might just be a bad story, a coping mechanism, a constant excuse to put out external fires when I had one smoldering inside me—and I was starting to choke.

The next morning, after sleeping in a hammock, I woke at dawn to the clicking and calling of geckos and blackbirds. Over coffee and breakfast tacos, I told my cousin Patty how guilty I felt about leaving my amazing staff, how sad I felt that I couldn't seem to turn it all around no matter how hard I tried, and also how utterly bone-tired I was. She looked at me and just listened quietly. And then I said something that surprised me: "I don't know, Patty, but it feels like there's more, like there's something deeper going on with me." I laid my palm over my heart.

"Can I give you a *limpia*?" she asked.

As she brushed a fresh bundle of basil down my body to sweep away bad energy, I finally burst into tears. I hadn't cried during all the stresses of work, even when I had to lay off my own friends. I didn't cry when I sent my mom money to put in my sister's commissary account so she could buy supplies in jail. And I didn't cry when Astrid, my younger daughter, accidentally hit me on my nose, which was still tender after falling off that barstool.

"What do you want to let go of?" Patty asked, brushing the fragrant plants across my chest. My guilt that I couldn't save everyone, my anger at myself for always wanting to try, and my ghostly sadness that always lied beneath. "Let it go," she whispered as she began to rub an egg over my body. "Let it go." Afterward, I walked two short blocks to the ocean, threw the herbs and egg into the great sea, and cleansed myself in the salt water.

Snuggling my feet into the warm sand in front of rolling blue-green waves, I opened a book and read something that changed my life. The book was *Woman Who Glows in the Dark* by Elena Avila, a well-known curandera. There I found the explanation for the never-ending ache I'd sought to fill with overpleasing and over-achieving. It was *susto*.

Though the literal translation of the Spanish word *susto* is "fright," the deeper meaning is "soul loss." In Curanderismo, susto is referred to as a "magical fright," similar to post-traumatic stress disorder. The idea of susto is that when something traumatic happens to you, a piece of your soul goes into hiding.

In the book, Avila describes soul loss as

a state in which we do not feel fully present or as if we are really ourselves. We experience a feeling that "something is missing" because our spirit, the energetic aura that surrounds us, has been violated. . . . In my culture, we have always known that the soul can be injured just as deeply as the body, mind, and emotions. We call this type of wounding *susto*. . . . Because the soul is sacred and should never be touched, when it is violated by traumatic experiences, it runs and hides, as if it had become frozen in time because of terrible events.[1]

"This is it!" I thought. "This is what I have!" Even under the shining sun, my whole body shivered at the recognition.

Soul loss.

What I had felt since my father's death. Without a guide and protector, I had tried my best to shepherd my sisters, mom, and myself. I had painted tough over the broken places. And with a blinding tenacity, I had set out and reached destinations I'd never imagined: New York City, the storied ladder of women's magazines, the set of the *Today* show, the new-releases table at Barnes & Noble, and even the White House.

I had tried so hard. I thought I'd beaten it.

And yet there I was, on the floor of a bar, bleeding all over myself. Susto. The world was slippery, but it was susto that pushed me over and knocked me down. It was susto that made me bleed.

"I don't want to fucking live like this anymore!" I said out loud. And I didn't want my sisters to live like this either. The truth was that in the three decades since my dad's death, we had suffered through addiction, incarceration, financial stress, and mental health challenges.

These were the issues we were always trying to raise awareness of at my job, problems like the Latina pay gap, the rapidly growing Latina incarceration rate, and the way-too-high Latina teen suicide rate. I'd been passionate about trying to serve my community—because I couldn't save my family.

My mind flashed to a memory of when I was thirteen, sitting next to Dad as he lay wasting away in a hospital. We both felt so helpless, we sat there saying nothing.

Susto.

I lost a piece of my soul that day. Susto.

The pain of being present with my own kids. Susto.

The wish to save everything in my path. Susto.

Drinking till I passed out, gone, gone, gone. Susto.

That need to stay busy so I never had to land, think, or feel. Susto.

But it wasn't just me. This trauma ran across generations. We were all suffering from susto—soul loss caused by inherited traumas and the lethal legacies of colonization, patriarchy, and systemic racism. And because we couldn't name it, we couldn't change it. So we just kept passing it down, generation to generation, like a tainted gift.

I let this powerful truth wash over me like the crashing waves. The only thing that kept my body anchored on that beach—instead of running to a bar or back to my phone with social media and all its steady drama—was the recognition that I needed my soul back.

I had to follow my susto to its root. It wasn't a coincidence Curanderismo had come back into my life. I didn't know exactly how, but I felt the ancestral medicine of my grandmothers would be my guide. I thought back to my cousins and aunt calling my name on the beach the day before. I'd felt as though I were in another world. According to Curanderismo, your name is connected to your soul. During a ritual called a "soul retrieval," a curandera will call your soul back to you until it is reintegrated, and you root back down in completion. I knew, down to my bones, that this was what I needed to do—without delay. In just a few months I would turn forty-five. I had been secretly dreading this birthday because forty-five was the age my father was when he was diagnosed with terminal cancer. At thirteen, it had seemed so far away, but now it was here, this macabre milestone. I was going to outlive my father.

I couldn't, and wouldn't, carry this susto any longer.

"Can I call back, unfreeze, and reclaim parts of myself so I can truly get rooted into the beauty of my life?" I wondered.

That morning, sitting on that beach, I made my decision. Not only could I—I had to.

Not finding a blueprint for how I could gather the lost pieces of myself back together again, like a Latina Humpty Dumpty, I began to create my own. I started jotting down ideas in my journal on the plane ride home. I wrote "Robyn's Reclamation Project" at the top of the page. Just seeing those words, I felt power and life surge back into me. I knew I was embarking on a serious and sacred—and possibly secret—mission. But how long would I give myself? Seized with the idea of going on a soul-retrieval journey, I began by researching time frames.

I discovered that the Mexica had two calendars.

One was 365 days, based on the solar cycle. But they also had another, more intriguing frame for time that ran 260 days. Called tōnalpōhualli, or "counting of the days," it was a "sacred almanac or divination calendar . . . used in casting horoscopes and interpreting the influences that affected . . . lives from birth to death."[2] The 260-day cycle signifies the creation and growth of humans. Its roughly nine-month time span is symbolic of the gestation period of a baby.

I began calculating. If I started on my birthday, June 11, which was weeks away, I'd end in late February. Looking at a calendar, I thought of my dad, who had died on Valentine's Day. Tracing my pen backward from that date—as if I could undo time—I stopped on May 31. When I had questioned my mom about my dad and his illness, the only date she could firmly recall was May 31, the day he'd been scheduled for emergency surgery. The attempt to remove all the cancer was unsuccessful, and the oncologist told my mother, "I'm sorry, but your husband only has one year to live."

He died on Valentine's Day, 260 days later.

I couldn't believe this connection. The chills I felt on the beach reading about susto were back. Something was happening. In the way that everything had spectacularly fallen apart, now it was all coming together. I felt like someone—my ancestors?—was leaving me clues.

I needed to keep following.

"Okay, two hundred sixty days, then," I said to myself or to whoever was listening.

I would take 260 days to heal, to retrieve my soul.

Sketching an outline of what these next nine months would look like, I wrote down a list of things I wanted to do, to reclaim, to learn, and to let go of. "I want to learn more about my dad," I wrote. Who was he? I had my memories, but what more could I learn about who he was as a person? I really didn't know much about his childhood. And I rarely talked about him to my kids. I didn't even have a photo up of him. That had to change.

"I want to learn about Mama Natalia." Mama Natalia was my maternal great-grandmother and a curandera. I remember going to her house when I was a kid, loving the smells from her cozy kitchen, but she spoke only Spanish, and I just smiled and ran around with my cousins, not paying attention. I yearned to learn more.

Thinking of Mama Natalia's fresh tortillas brought another area I wanted to focus on: cooking. I was a pretty terrible cook, mostly because I was usually so busy, I'd rush through everything— including meal prep. In addition to being a curandera, Mama

Natalia was a wonderful cook. In fact, the strongest memories I have are of her standing over a stove in her *mandil*, making hearty (and heart-comforting) dishes like *carne guisada* and *fideo*. Nowadays, my specialty was quesadillas. What would Mama Natalia say?

One of my favorite places in my town was a restaurant called Lupe's. I loved it because it was the best (and only) Mexican restaurant and because the owner, Lupe, and her daughter, Yesenia, treated me like family. Lupe had been telling me for months to come into the restaurant and take cooking classes with her. Now that I had time, could I (re)learn some traditional, healthy recipes and some culture along the way?

"Learn to cook traditional Mexican food" made the list.

I also added, "Get healthy." As part of health, I wanted to eat better, feel stronger, and learn more about Curanderismo. I knew I needed to slow down and reconnect with my body and this sacred medicine. And I also wanted to spread this connection to Mother Earth. Many practicing curanderos were skilled herbalists. We had our own garden, though it was mostly Lars who tended to it. I looked out the window at the garden and wrote, "Study plant medicine."

As I considered more things to embrace and overhaul, "finances" made the list. I had always had a somewhat unhealthy relationship with money.

My mother's attitude had been, "We're poor, and we'll always be poor."

As a teenager, I cringed and yelled back, "Speak for yourself, woman!" But when I thought about it, the truth was I was more like her than I wanted to admit. I had very little personal savings and was a chronic undercharger for my work. In fact, at my last job, I earned way under market value and paid for many things, like staff lunches and video equipment, out of my own pocket—often not getting paid back because I lost receipts or turned in expenses too late.

In one true show of how I undervalued myself, my copresident and I were working side-by-side once when he looked at my computer and laughed. One column of my screen was all white because the light was burning out. I worked like this, with a broken screen, while he was working on a brand-new MacBook.

"Ask for a new computer!" he chastised. But I never did. New computers were always in demand—as writers and digital creatives, we couldn't live without them—yet I felt guilty for taking the best ones. So here I was, the copresident of the company, with the busted computer.

I knew I wasn't alone in my relationship with money. Women still made less than men, and women of color made less than anyone else in America, with Latinas and Native American women rounding out the bottom, earning just fifty-seven cents to the dollar a white man makes. Why was that? Yes, there were definitely institutional things at play, but what else? What was I not asking for? What was I not valuing in myself?

"Rediscover my worth," I wrote.

Then I added two things I knew were tied in with this: "be a more attentive parent, partner, and friend" and "redefine success." I needed to make money, but the way I'd been working wasn't sustainable, and I could never put work in front of my family or friendships again.

"Okay, what else do I really want to do?" I asked.

"Save my sisters," I wrote. No, scratch that. No more saving. "Reconnect with my sisters."

And I added, "Practice Curanderismo," even though it made me nervous even to wish for.

At the end I wrote, "Heal my soul, bring it back."

I looked at my list, the new map I had sketched out for myself. For too long, I think my susto had been in charge. Now it was time to let something else be my guide. I was scared and fragile, but I was ready to get rooted.

Everything was good, serendipitous, meant to be! Until my loving and ever-practical husband dropped me back to earth.

"So you're not getting a new job?" Lars asked.

"I'm gonna freelance," I said. "I am going to be working; I'm just not going to take another full-time gig right now."

I had already been offered a few positions after I left the company, but I couldn't jump on another runaway train. I tried to explain this to Lars.

"Babe, I am burnt the fuck out," I said. Then I added a truer truth. "And honestly, something is going on with me. If I take another full-time job, I'm just gonna do the same thing again: work like a maniac, never be here for you and the kids, drink too much. I need to fix whatever is going on."

He looked at me, worried, so I added quickly, "I'm good, babe," reassuring him and maybe lying. "But I wanna be great—for us."

"New book?" he asked, embracing me.

When Lars and I met, we were both well into our thirties, with a lot of life under our belts. Our coming together was what we had called "a new book," meaning we'd always try to be fresh and open with each other.

"New book," I said, hugging him back tightly, steadying myself against his warmth and praying I was doing the right thing.

That night, as Lars watched *Frozen* with the girls, I sat upstairs in my office and lit a bundle of dried sage. It was day one of my reclamation project, and I wanted to mark the moment—to acknowledge the journey I was embarking on. I had learned in the Curanderismo class that before you begin a soul retrieval, you call in "the Five Directions."

You begin by praying toward each direction, starting in the east, the land of new beginnings, where the sun rises. In this direction, you pray for new dreams and possibilities.

Looking out my window toward what I thought was east at a towering Douglas fir, I blurted out to whoever was listening, "Look, universe, I need a healing. I've been through some shit, as you might already know, and I need help. Like *major* help. I'm so grateful for Lars and my girls, and I loved my job, but I don't know what happened. I got lost somewhere along the way. I just want to feel good, to be at peace. And I want to know myself again. I want to *like* myself again. And I want my sisters to be happy and healthy and the way we used to be. If that's even possible?"

After a moment, I looked out to the mountains in the west. In this direction, where the sun sets, is where things die and are reborn. Here, you let go of the old so you can create space for the new. "There's so much I want to let go of," I whispered. Praying to the west, I asked, "Can you please take away the awful guilt I have for leaving my position, ignoring my kids, and basically letting everyone down?" I was about to turn to the next direction when I had one last thought. "And please! Can you help me drop this scary idea that I'm no one without my job?"

Feeling embarrassed to be talking out loud but also relieved, I looked out at the large, darkened sky to the north. The north symbolizes the past and the place of our ancestors. Here you call on family members to help guide you. A huge part of this journey of healing and reclamation I was embarking on was to get to know my ancestors, like Mama Natalia, la curandera. But who knew what other chingonas might be in the mix?

Closing my eyes, I took a deep breath and imagined my father the way he was before he was ravaged by pancreatic cancer. I started to tear up as I saw his earthy brown eyes, and I felt a knock in my chest from a place that had felt too long hollow. "Hi, Dad," I said softly.

Next, I tried to visualize Mama Natalia. The memories I had of her were faint. But soon, with focus, I began to remember what she looked like when I was a kid: wrinkly, sweet, and old, old, old, like Mamá Coco in the Disney movie. "Hi, Mama Natalia," I said tentatively, squeezing my eyes shut so the image wouldn't go away. "I'm really excited to get to know you, to learn about your life and your gifts. I am hoping to maybe be a curandera too, like you. Can you come be with me and guide me to help me find my way?" I felt the evening breeze blow in from the open window, and I took that as a yes.

With that off my chest, I felt ready to face the south. This direction is symbolic of children, willpower, and courage. In my mom's house hangs a giant photo of me at age three wearing a yellow sun-dress with messy pigtails. I have always loved that photo. I imag-ined little me now.

"Don't worry, sweetie," I said to myself. "I'm coming for you."

There is also a fifth direction that represents community. You get there after you pass through the other four directions, having completed the circle. This last direction reminds us that we are all connected. In that moment, conjuring the strength of ones who passed so I could change the path for the ones to come, I felt a stir-ring: hope.

Get Rooted Practice #1
Orient Yourself

Before we set out on our journey, it's important that we take a moment to orient ourselves, to stop and look around and take stock of where we are, where we came from, and where we want to go. We call on the Five Directions to help us do that. The energy of each cardinal point—the east, west, north, and south—helps guide us. They give us strength to draw on and a compass to help us steer our path.

To begin your work with the Five Directions, sit in a cozy, quiet place, and center yourself. You can do some calming breath work, or light some candles or incense—whatever you need to create an atmosphere of quiet and contemplation. In a journal, take some time to write down your hopes for each direction.*

Start in the east, the place of beginnings and freshness. Here we call in the essence** of Quetzalcoatl, who represents learning and knowledge. In your journal, write down what you want to invite into your life and what you hope to learn on this journey. The east is our intention. And with our intentions, we create direction.

Next move to the west, which is ruled by Xipe Totec, the energy of spring and renewal. This is the direction of letting go. The symbol is an ear of corn, whose kernels you reveal only after you peel away the husks. Write down all the things you are ready to release: feelings, situations, maybe even people. You don't have to *do* anything at this moment. Just getting it out on paper is a powerful unburdening.

---

* The interpretations of the meaning of the directions, their assigned guardians, and associated elements vary widely, but I am presenting the way that I learned from maestra Virgina Rincón, who was a student of Elena Avila and whom I followed on this journey.

** I have learned that Precontact, the Indigenous peoples of Mexico did not have a concept of "God" but instead considered guardians like Quetzalcoatl not as deities but more like energies, essences, or forces of nature.

When you are done, it's time for the north: the place of ancestors. Tezcatlipoca, the Smoking Mirror, rules the night sky. Who in your lineage do you hope to learn more about? Your resilient abuela or rebellious aunt? Write a little note to them introducing yourself and begin planning your steps to discover more about them—and you.

Next, call in the south, the direction of willpower and children. The south is guarded by Huitzilopochtli, also called the Hummingbird on the Left, who symbolizes the sun, but also our hearts, which lie in the south and left of our chests. What do you hope to reclaim? Your childhood dreams that you abandoned in adulthood? The confidence and ease you had as a kid? The south reminds us of the belief of a child and our own indomitable will to rise with eternal love, light, and joy.

Last, the fifth direction is about community and connection. It is supported by the directions and intentions you just set. I have no doubt you'll call on your comadres and community to help you as you travel. But the most important connection you'll make on this journey is with yourself.

We finish by honoring Tonatiuh, Father Sky; Tonantzin, Mother Earth; and then our own *corazón*. So for now, place your hand on your heart and take a moment to listen to its steady beat.

Thank yourself for having the courage to take this journey.

2

Moving the Winds

"Babe!" Lars called as I walked outside toward our garden, where he and Lucia and Astrid were watering poppies. "I want to show you something."

"Mama, come see!" Lucia chimed in. As they pointed to a fresh spot in our flower bed, I knew instantly what they were going to say. "Someone buried an egg in our garden," said Lars, totally bewildered. "I saw something sticking out, and at first I thought a bird made a nest, but it's a chicken egg! It's so weird." He bent over and unearthed the brown egg.

"Egg, Mama," chimed in Astrid, as mesmerized as if she were watching a magic act.

"Um . . . yeah, I put it there," I said, trying to act as if this was all totally normal. I pointed to where velvety sage and spiky rosemary were overtaking the basil. "There's one over there too."

"What the heck?" asked Lucia. It was her new favorite expression. As Lucia and her sidekick ran to dig for the other egg I'd buried, I answered my husband's questioning look. "I gave Astrid and me a limpia the other day."

"And?" he asked.

"You use an egg for spiritual cleansing, and then you can bury it."

His raised eyebrows refused to lower with comprehension.

"You know, so the earth can absorb all the negative energy," I said. "I thought our garden was a good place."

Lars looked at me as if I'd told him I laid that egg myself. Then he laughed and said, "What the heck?"

Setting out on my healing journey, I had felt determined, inspired, and ready. But now, a week after sending a desperate prayer to the Five Directions, the dust had settled. My phone, which used to ring and ping with *important* business, now lay unnervingly silent. And after Lars went to work and I dropped the kids off, I'd grab my coffee and sit alone in my garden. Just me, my sage, and my whopping insecurity.

I had told very few people about my reclamation project, and I felt as though I were in the first trimester of a pregnancy. I was still super unsure how all this was gonna pan out, and I didn't feel like sending out the shower invites. Also, I didn't want to be colored by anyone's opinion—which people *always* have.

Literally minutes after I resigned from my job, all anyone wanted to know was what I was doing next. What I *felt* like doing was going nowhere and dissolving—like the caterpillar before it becomes the butterfly. Except I didn't even want to be the butterfly. I just wanted to wrap myself up and fall apart for a while. This genuinely didn't seem bad to me, but almost no one could handle the in-between, can't-put-a-name-on-it life I was living. Our society doesn't seem to value or support any sort of pause. Add to that the "mystical" quality of my Curanderismo studies, and many people would just write me off as having a midlife crisis, as one friend bluntly suggested. So I was keeping a lid on it all for now, which made me feel really lonely.

But as I turned my attention to my Curanderismo studies, I began to understand this hopeful/uncertain phase was a hallmark feeling of the east, where you usually start your healing journey. Because no matter how lousy—or slippery—our day is, a bigger force helps us turn the page. And it happens each and every day: the sunrise.

The Mexica believed there was magic in the sunrise and used it as a metaphor for rebirth[1] and starting fresh. That's exactly what I needed: a fresh start. Just as a good gust of wind cleans away debris and dirt before spring planting, I decided to channel this cleansing energy by sweeping and cleaning my house and clearing the space in my head and heart via the act of a limpia.

In Spanish, *limpia* means to clean, but in Curanderismo, a limpia is an energetic cleansing to remove dense or stuck emotions, creating new pathways and possibilities. Limpias are what people call on curanderas for the most. Patty had given me that amazing limpia in Mexico using fresh basil and an egg, and I had felt so calm and clear afterward. You can get a limpia for pretty much everything, from the ending of a relationship to clearing away bad vibes after spending time with a stressed-out or jealous person.

I began to practice self-limpia by cleansing myself with my sage bundle in the mornings as I tried to get back into my meditation practice.

Later in the week, while everyone was at work and school, I took a leisurely walk down to a local acupuncturist who was selling mugwort smoke bundles. I had read that popular cleansing tools like white sage and palo santo sticks were becoming overharvested,[2] so, trying to be ecologically conscious and culturally respectful, some people had begun to use local herbs, which, for me, meant mugwort. Mugwort grows abundantly in the wild where I live. It borders my own yard and is called a "dream weed" because it's supposed to invoke dreaming and divination. After spending some time chatting with Masha the acupuncturist, I paid her ten dollars and headed home with my new gift.

When I returned, I lit my mugwort bundle and sat transfixed by the billowing plumes, making wavy and winding shapes as they blew upward, disappearing into the air. The smoke smelled much sweeter than sage and reminded me of marijuana.

Compared to the other elements—fierce fire, magical water, and sacred earth—my Gemini airiness always felt a little . . . light. But as I exhaled and felt my body relax and inhaled the fragrant herbs, I considered how potent air actually is. In the Bible, our spirit is referred to as "breath of God," filling and reviving. I thought about the magic of a chant, the fervent hope of a whispered prayer, the weight of a stated intention. Air is also a force that can cleanse and destroy, like a mighty storm. As I inhaled a renewing deep breath, I felt new appreciation for my airy self. Not as someone who could fly away, but as someone who could root into my breath, inhale into my strength, and channel the winds.

The Mexica were famed for their cleanliness. When the Spanish arrived at Tenochtitlan in ancient Mexico, they were astonished by the clean streets, fresh water, and impeccable personal hygiene of the people they encountered.[3] The Mexica associated cleanliness with order and stability, but it also had a spiritual purpose. Brooms had great metaphorical qualities for the Mexica. Not only would the brooms restore calm and balance in the home, but the Mexica believed that the act of sweeping invites newness and beginnings.[4] My life coaching instructor once said that the universe wants to deliver everything you want, but it can only be delivered to your true home: where peace lives. Limpia and cleaning bring peace.

I was searching hard for that peace as I sorted through piles and piles of stuff.

In a corner of my closet was a giant stack of old magazines with my byline. I sat down and looked at the covers I had helped choose and the stories I had written. There was a photo of me with one of my editor's letters, sitting on a velvet couch in fabulous cobalt-blue heels. It was a little over the top, but the shoes were beautiful, the couch was beautiful—hell, the whole magazine was beautiful! And I had been *la jefa*, the editor in chief. That was a big achievement for a little girl from San Antonio.

I was overcome with a rush of pride. My job had become messy in the end, but it still had been gorgeous and fun and so very worthy. I tried to remember that as I recycled many old issues—but not all. I wanted to save some to show to the girls one day. My colleagues and I had worked hard at this, and I could say goodbye to what was no longer needed while holding on to the good.

The east is a place of mystery; we never know what the new day will bring. I felt this acutely as I swept my office and dragged my desk to an area with better light. Looking out over the fir tree, I didn't know what my next career move would be or how this project would pan out, but I felt the winds moving.

As I continued doing limpia, opening the windows of my house and heart, I felt ready to invite someone important in: my great-grandmother Mama Natalia.

Abuelita, as we called her, died at the age of eighty-six, when I was nine years old. To find out more about her, I call up my great-aunt Dora. At ninety-two, Dora was the oldest living relative in my family and the person who could share about Mama Natalia the best because she lived with her growing up.

"*Mija! ¿Cómo estás?*" exclaimed Dora brightly when I rang her at her home in Killeen, Texas. She sounded as vibrant and delightful as ever. Getting straight to the point, I said, "Dora, I'm calling because I've heard from my mom that 'uelita was a curandera. Is that true?"

Dora didn't miss a beat. "Yes, mija. She had 'the gift.' Many, many people would come visit Mama Natalia to have their cards read," she said. "They would pay whatever they could afford, a few dollars or even a bag of rice." Mama Natalia had clients who paid her in cash and in tamales and tortillas, and she treated them all the same. According to Dora, Mama Natalia was very popular and had regular customers who came to her for weekly sessions, just like a therapist. "One wealthy lady wouldn't do anything in her business without consulting Mama Natalia first!" Dora told me proudly.

Hearing this made me feel as though I'd found buried treasure beneath my house. I stood up from my lawn chair and started looking around my backyard for someone, *anyone*, to tell. Seeing only birds and a pacing squirrel did nothing to diminish my excitement.

It's said that most curanderos have the *don,* or gift, of healing, though most curanderos will tell you that God is the ultimate healer. Curanderos consider themselves vessels, or *cajitas*—"little boxes"—that divine spirit comes through to heal.[5] Regardless of someone's personal spiritual beliefs, anyone can benefit from the practices of Curanderismo as long as they believe in the possibility of healing.

"What would they come to her for?" I asked, hungry for details.

"Well," Dora said slowly, calling forth memories from decades ago, "she would treat *mal de ojo, este . . . empacho . . .* and *. . . susto.*"

I put her on mute and actually screamed, "Holy shit!" The birds and the squirrel went running.

Along with susto, mal de ojo and empacho are other common folk illnesses recognized in Curanderismo. Hearing Dora say these words, terms I'd only read in my books, felt as though I had finally walked through the right door. In layman's terms, *mal de ojo* translates to the "illness caused by staring"[6] and is recognized all over the world as the "evil eye" or a curse someone can give you with their powerful, evil glare. Amulets and talismans like the *hamsa,* a hand with an eye in the center, are thought to ward off evil.

In Curanderismo, mal de ojo is a little different and lighter in scope. It's most often referred to as an illness affecting babies and children who have been too fawned over or stared at.

Dora recalled a time when her own daughter got mal de ojo. "Once, I had Rachel dressed all nice, and a lady came selling ice cream. I bought Rachel a cone, and the lady kept saying how cute she was. *'¡Qué chula, qué chula!'* Thirty minutes later, Rachel broke into convulsions!"

Terrified, Dora ran to Mama Natalia, who told her how to heal Rachel with an egg. "I rubbed it over her little body while saying a prayer, cracked the egg open into a glass of water, and put it under the bed. Within an hour, she was fine."

Another common illness that Mama Natalia treated was empacho. Empacho comes from the verb *empachar,* which means to be stopped up, like with indigestion, and is considered some type of blockage, which can be physical or mental. According to Dora,

Mama Natalia used to treat empacho by having the person drink an herbal tea like manzanilla—chamomile. She also massaged them and, according to Dora, "pinched the skin along the spine until it popped, and the empacho would come out." I remember my mom telling me that when she was young and her and her sisters' stomachs hurt, Mama Natalia massaged their little bellies with olive oil so their aches and constipation would go away.

Through Dora's recollections, I felt Mama Natalia growing from a faint memory to a person I could fully imagine, and for the first time since I quit my job, I felt like I could finally breathe.

As I continued my house limpia, I eyed our bar cart and knew there was something else I needed to cleanse: my body. If I truly wanted to care for myself, I could not consume alcohol during these 260 days. Though I had definitely tapered off after falling off that barstool, I hadn't quit completely.

The phrase *clean and sober* came to mind, but that felt a little too intense. I did, however, like the idea of being *clear and cleansed* through this process. If the next nine months of this healing journey would feel something like a pregnancy and rebirth, then I should be sober, like when I was pregnant.

I was also spurred by the fact that curanderas often recommend not drinking alcohol or eating meat in the days before a cleansing. They believed that would improve people's energy and make healings easier. To make things official, I took bottles from our bar down into the basement so they'd be out of sight and hopefully out of mind. Lars wasn't a big drinker. But for me, it felt like a needed move in the right direction.

At dinner that night—where I drank kombucha instead of wine—I was excited to tell Lars about my conversation with Dora. "I was talking to my great-aunt for my project. She's ninety-two!" I told him as I served Lucia and Astrid rice, beans, and quesadillas, which was the extent of my "Mexican" cooking. "She told me Mama Natalia, my great-grandmother, was definitely . . . a curandera!"

"A what?" said Lucia.

"A healer," I replied.

"A what?" asked Astrid.

"Someone who heals you with plants and prayer, and maybe magic?" I said, trying to explain something I was just beginning to understand myself.

"A witch?" asked little Astrid.

"Um, not exactly," I said, thinking of how people often called Curanderismo *brujería* when they wanted to dismiss it. "But someone who *could* make magical potions and cure you."

"Like a doctor witch!" said Lucia, interrupting me as her eyes got really big. She looked at Astrid, and they both started laughing.

"Was she a hundred?" asked Lucia, who, at age six, thought one hundred was ancient.

"No, she was eighty-six."

Then Astrid got serious and said, "Witches and ghosts are weal."

"Yes, they are!" I said emphatically, while Lars and Lucia—the skeptics—both looked at me as if I were wearing a black pointy hat myself.

"You know what I was thinking?" I announced, about to suggest we do a new craft box after dinner. It had glow-in-the-dark projects, and I was feeling magical.

"That you want a new full-time job?" said Lars.

"*No,*" I said loudly. "Do you want me to be gone all the time again?"

"I'm just kidding," Lars said quickly, though I didn't think he was. "What were you gonna say?"

Not wanting to fight, I started clearing the table and said in a forced cheery voice, "Let's do the glow-in-the-dark craft box! Y'all want to?"

"Yay!" screamed the girls.

"Okay, wash your hands, and we'll come out and set it up."

Sensing I was upset, Lars followed me into the kitchen. "I was just kidding," he said. "I don't want you to go back to work in the city. It's nice having you here. We need you."

"I know," I murmured as I cuddled into his chest. "I need a break," I said, still hugging him and looking way up into his eyes. At six foot two, he's nearly a foot taller than me. "*And* I need to work on my project. It's important to me."

"I know," he said softly, laying his chin on my head.

"It will be hard, moneywise, but we'll just dial back. We can do it!"

Lars didn't reply. He kissed me on my head and went out to clear our table for the project.

Lars is the earth to my air, the rock to my roll, but we couldn't be more different. He is a software engineer who thrives in systems and organization and has worked for the same company for eighteen years. My chaotic upbringing meant I was very comfortable and familiar with change, which had made me really daring, and I would pretty much try anything once. My past gigs included working the desk at a yoga studio, selling cookware on the QVC television network, and co-owning a vintage store. Yet Lars and I fit, the way the sun nestled into the crescent moon in one of my favorite necklaces. Our love was based less on trying to be on the same page and way more on accepting each other exactly as we were, which was one of our wedding vows.

But as I turned to the messy stack of dishes in the sink, I could feel the pressure—external and internal—to do something, to earn my keep. I was still working every day, not only on freelance work to cover my bills, but on healing myself, which I knew in my core I needed desperately. Yet, it felt weird not to have my identity tied to a job or a title. I was even calling this healing journey a "project," so it seemed more legit and useful. I sensed on a deep level that it was important to untether myself from this caricatured #momboss hustler persona. But then who would I be?

As I was loading the dishwasher, I thought of Mama Natalia. In addition to all the fantastical stuff she did, she was, at her essence, a working mom. She'd been widowed at forty-one, left to take care of her three kids by working as a baker and seamstress by day and a curandera at night and on weekends—reading people's fortunes and administering remedies. "I wonder if people thought she was eccentric," I asked myself. "I wonder if she had time to care," was my answer.

As I looked at my own sweet family putting together our STEM project on our dining table, I thought for the first time not only of Mama Natalia's healing ways but of how she handled her life. "It's hard out here for a healer," I thought as I went to help Lars unpack the craft box so we could teach our girls the magic of luminescence.

Later that evening, I was reading a book on Aztec philosophy when I heard Astrid screaming in a nightmare. I stayed with her, rocking her quietly until she gradually calmed down. That's when she hiccuped, "Why . . . don't . . . you . . . like . . . me?"

I felt as if someone had punched me in the chest. "I love you, Astrid! Why do you say that?"

"Because you didn't ask me!" she cried.

"Ask you what?" I said desperately.

"You know what *ask* means!" she screamed accusingly. She must have still been dreaming.

So I cradled her tight, murmuring, "I love you, my baby, my baby. You're safe, my baby." Soon she fell asleep. Wanting to take her scary dreams away and still feeling the energy of my conversation with Dora earlier, I ran downstairs and grabbed a carton of eggs. I passed one slowly over her body, intently saying a prayer. When I was done, I grabbed another egg, running it over mine from head to toe, exhaling to release my stress and fear. Afterward, I crawled in bed next to her, and as she nestled in my arm, I fell asleep and dreamed that I was falling and falling.

The next morning, I woke up exhausted. I took the egg carton downstairs to the kitchen along with the two eggs I'd used and placed those next to the compost bucket. After a limpia, some people break the eggs into a glass of water, as Dora had described, and "read" the contents to see if someone sent you bad energy or to determine the cause of your troubles. But some curanderos kept the egg whole after a limpia and buried it. Looking over at Astrid, who was bright and chipper eating a bagel, I picked up the still-intact eggs holding our bad juju and decided to just throw them away. I already suspected what was bothering Astrid. And even though she was happy all morning, after dropping her off at day care, I sat in the car and cried. Her words lodged into a hole in my chest.

"Why don't you like me? Why didn't you ask me?"

When I had started my last job, Astrid hadn't even been a year old. Initially, I was only supposed to work two days a week in the office as a freelance editor, as my commute was two hours each way. But as I got promoted each year, the responsibility, and time away from family, grew to me going to the office five days a week and working 24-7. I always felt that, as the baby, Astrid had borne the brunt of that. I'd felt as if I'd dumped her off at day care and come back for her three years later.

"Why don't you like me? Why didn't you ask me?"

The truth is that she could have just been dreaming. But what I *felt* was that she was telling me to pay more attention—to her and to everything in my life.

Later that day, I looked at a beautiful old black-and-white photo of Mama Natalia I had placed on my altar. I picked up the photo and ran my finger over the image of her hair in a bun and her graceful, clasped hands. Three kids, three jobs, and no husband. Yet she looked peaceful here. "How did you do it?" I asked aloud. "How did you not fall apart?" I looked into her soulful eyes. "How did you put yourself back together?"

Mama Natalia's mother died when she was very young, and her father left her and her brother with relatives before moving back to Mexico. Dora told me that when Mama Natalia married my great-grandfather, Papa Julio, at just fourteen, and finally had a house of her own, she painstakingly created the beautiful environment she had never known growing up. She diligently washed their curtains and scrubbed the floors by hand because she did a better job than any mop.

Thinking about Mama Natalia as I was tidying up the girls' room, I wondered if maybe my great-grandma had been rubbing out bad memories and watching the sad things she experienced as a lonely kid flow down the drain, wrung free from her cleaning rag. By caring for her home, Mama Natalia was intentionally moving the winds away from her sad childhood toward the loving and ordered space she created for her children.

I felt a kinship with her as I tried to move my own parenting winds from absence to attention. We call these acts "cleaning." But what we are really doing is *righting* things, aren't we? Putting back in place the things that had come undone somewhere long ago.

I was trying to put things back in order in my kitchen cabinets later in the week when Dora called to talk about Mama Natalia and susto. To heal susto, according to Dora, Mama Natalia did something I hadn't read about in any of my books: "She would sweep them with *alumbre*," explained Dora. Alumbre, a crystalline stone, is known as fire rock. It's similar to what many people use as a natural deodorant. "After a limpia, Mama Natalia would heat the alumbre in a skillet until it got soft, creating a shadow or shape revealing what caused the susto. Then, she would pray over the person, saying aloud their name: '*Regresa*, Robyn, *regresa*! Come back, Robyn, come back!' Calling their soul back home."

Though I didn't fully understand yet how Mama Natalia's methods worked, I was utterly astonished to hear about them. Mama Natalia had healed susto. The question was, could I?

Later, when I was making dinner, my mom called to give me an update on my older sister. Lety had struggled with substance use for years but had recently gotten sober. Through her recovery program, she'd applied for a job refilling greeting card racks at drugstores. She had been hired and was so excited. But they rescinded the offer because she was still on probation.

My mom said Lety was doing well and applying for colleges, but the shame and stigma she felt about her past weighed heavily on her. Though I now had way more time on my hands, I'd been avoiding calling Lety because I didn't know how to help.

For the longest time, I thought a curandera meant someone who *cured*. I think that's why I resisted the call of Curanderismo—because it felt so intimidating. But recently I came across another meaning for the word *cura*, and that is to care for. I didn't know whether I would ever feel ready to cure anyone. But I was trying my best to care for Lars and the girls—and myself. Maybe I could try to care for my sisters and mom.

That I *could* do.

The next day, I was loading the dishwasher when I noticed the two brown eggs that I had used for Astrid's and my limpia still sitting next to the compost. I grabbed both the compost and eggs and walked outside. As I emptied the organic waste into our outside bin, it occurred to me that we spend so much time avoiding the messes in our lives because it all feels so daunting. But maybe it doesn't have to be so complicated. When crisis strikes, when all feels lost and you can't make one more damn decision, maybe you just move toward what you *can* do. Pick up a broom, pass the egg, wipe the dusty window—with simple and holy care.

If we could approach the messy people and places in our lives with the humble willingness to support instead of the obsessive need to fix, then we might find that the caring becomes the cure.

I went into the garden and placed my hands in the cool earth of my flower bed. I scooped out the moist dirt, gently plopping the eggs into the holes I had dug. Covering them, I felt a soft breeze blow on my neck. I sat back on my heels, looking up at the sky. The girls ran out, calling me to play. It was time for a new beginning.

Get Rooted Practice #2
Moving the Winds Limpia Meditation

There are limpia practices that work with every element—water, fire, earth, and air—and enough ways to work with each element to fill an entire book. But as an air sign, I really love working with the power of wind.

Moving the winds,* which works by intentionally blowing away—and clearing out—undesired moods, energies, emotions, habits, channels, and ways of being, is something I do regularly through my own breath work, through limpia with smoke medicine or an egg,**7 and even by cleansing myself in a gust of wind.

Once, a beloved family member was in critical condition in the ICU, every day their survival unsure. Each morning before I walked through the sliding glass hospital doors into that cold, beeping, and scary place, I paused at the hospital entrance portico, which acted like a wind tunnel. I'd let the gusty breeze whip through me, blowing away my choking fear and allowing me to collect myself before I walked through those doors and into the uncertainty that lay beyond.

Performing self-limpia is a good practice to blow away negative energies and interactions of the day so they don't stack up and weigh you down. I created this wind meditation to help you create your own self-limpia practice. You may want to record yourself reading this meditation and play it back or visit www.robyn moreno.com/meditation for more meditations.

To begin, sit in a comfortable position. Start to deepen your breathing.

---

* I first became familiar with "moving the winds" when I took a class on the four elements with maestra Alma and her partner, Xolot.

** The practice of cleansing with a raw egg has been handed down across generations, though its exact origins are unknown. Some scholars cite Spanish influence, but a research paper I found suggests that egg limpias have more African contributions than European, noting the practice of sweeping with eggs and chickens found in West African healing rituals.

Exhaling, we blow away what we no longer need. Inhaling, we breathe in the fresh air of hope and possibility.

Bring your attention to the crown of your head. Imagine a cleansing wind as it begins to circle, sweeping out any tightness, any thoughts, any anxieties.

We feel the dissipation, and as we exhale, we feel the release.

We feel movement as a cleansing breeze moves across our face, softening our brow, unclenching our jaw.

We feel cleansing air move around our throats, removing the need to speak when we don't want to and giving us the will to speak when we do, so we can find words of comfort for ourselves and others.

We imagine the cleansing winds move down over our neck and shoulders and feel the unburdening. We exhale relaxation. We don't have to carry the world.

We feel the soothing air move down our capable arms. The arms we use to hold each other. The arms we use to carry. As we feel the breeze blow down our arms, it takes away the aches and the hurt. And it moves down and out our fingertips and flows straight to Tonantzin, Mother Earth.

Now, we feel the cleansing winds blow through our chests, our open hearts. We release any sadness, and if it comes forth in tears, we welcome that. That just means that we feel, and it flows in all the places and through all the rivers, healing all the brokenness—again and again.

We feel the calming wind energy come down our backs. Our strong backs are where the ancestors live, moving the line forward.

We inhale recognition, and as we exhale, we imagine ourselves letting go, falling backward, and being held by generation after generation of hands that are always waiting to hold us. A soft back means that we are held—and we can do that.

We bring awareness now to our solar plexus, the seat of our will. Here we let go of any forcing. Any demanding. Any unnecessary have-tos or shoulds. We feel the tightness on the inhale, and exhale to only what is.

We feel the winds move down to our hips: the place of birthing, the place of the grandmothers. Mother after mother, generation after generation. They're telling us, "We've been here, mija; we know this struggle. You can give it to us now." We move down, moving away any fear, any doubts, any uncertainty, leaving only the recollection of our resilience that resides in our bones.

We feel the soothing air move down our muscular legs that carry us, that are taut with power, that allow us to run and play. We are discerning with our power: we stand when we need to; we stand for others. And we sit when we are ready.

We imagine the winds move down our legs, down our ankles, and through the feet, which connect us to the earth. It's all released to Tonantzin, Mother Earth. She accepts it all and says, "Thank you, thank you for coming back to me again and again."

And in this place of flow and freedom, we say a prayer that is lifted high in the sky, carried above our houses and cities and rivers and trees and oceans and across the universe. And that prayer says, "I love you."

3

Is It Susto or Ser?

I really hoped a worm wouldn't crawl in my hair.

After a few stressful weeks involving work and family drama and decisions I wasn't ready to make, I knelt in the woods near my house, staring into a six-inch hole. I had dug this small grave with my own bare hands, scooping out moist chunks of dirt by the handful, working through leaves and rocks, and then roots.

I looked into that hollowed-out space, then around, making sure no hikers were watching me, and leaned my body over the pit. Taking a breath and silently praying no bugs would come slithering out, I stuck my face into the hole in the fresh earth. Into that cool darkness, the tightness I had been carrying in my chest bubbled up and out in fury. I began to scream.

Just a few weeks into my reclamation project, and shit was getting real. After I had spent weeks learning about Mama Natalia, doing a limpia on my life, and finally giving myself permission to take time to care for me and family, an unexpected message threatened to blow it all up.

I hadn't checked my email in a while because no one was really calling, so I was curious to find a notification from LinkedIn. I opened it and saw that it was a headhunter from a digital kitchen brand looking for a VP of content. Food and recipes were always the most popular sections of the site and magazine I used to run, and I loved home content. I had been a lifestyle editor for years.

I had just told Lars I wasn't looking for full-time work because I was committed to freelancing while I healed my heart and home, but curious (and honestly flattered) that someone reached out, I agreed to chat with the HR person—and she was pretty flippin' awesome.

She was a fellow woman of color and spoke glowingly about this new potential gig. My ears perked up when she said it was financially stable and listed as one of the fastest-growing companies in America. She talked extensively about the generous benefits that included gym and fitness classes. And she mentioned stock options, as well as "frequent giveaways and treats from our test kitchen." She almost had me at "treats from our test kitchen" when she mentioned the salary range. That's when I almost dropped the phone. It was more than I had made at my last job. In fact, it would be the highest salary I had made to date.

After she was done with her pitch, she asked if I had any questions. I asked about diversity at the company and about the company culture. Then I let her know honestly that I had left my last job partly because I had very young children and my schedule was overloaded.

"You do have to come into the New York office," she said when I floated the idea of working all-remote. "But," she continued, "most of the directors are parents, and there are rarely late nights." She finished by saying, "Robyn, I really connected with your digital editorial experience, and I loved what you did at your last job. Our future here is very bright, and I really think you'd be a great fit and asset."

I hung up after agreeing to a follow-up interview.

"Shit," I thought.

Were the universe and Mama Natalia testing me? I was confused. I knew Lars would want me to take it. And if I reached out to any of my friends, most (if not all) would tell me to take the job.

In fact, some branding expert who I sat next to at a "power luncheon"—that a dear friend invited me to, I think because she felt sorry for me—told me with complete authority that I should act fast, "go big," and strike while the iron was hot workwise while people still associated me with my last job. "Don't take too much time," she warned me when I responded truthfully about my decision to take a pause to gather myself and spend more time with my children. "It gets harder to get a good position the longer you are unemployed," she said. "People forget about you."

Yikes. That sounded dire.

Maybe I *was* getting off-track and weird in my solitude out here in the country with just my family and Curanderismo books and way too many anxious thoughts. Maybe going back to work would be good for me, get me back in the game? Give me some direction? Keep me busy? Give me money to help Lars and my family?

"This could be good," I said to myself as I looked toward the east and over the Douglas fir, a direction I had been looking toward a lot lately. This position would give me an opportunity to lead a team again, and this time have the resources to execute my vision. "I have taken a pretty decent break," I thought. I was feeling more energized and clearer. Maybe it was time to move these winds back into making money, using my talents, and being the badass I knew myself to be. Then my eyes landed on my driveway with purple Rollerblades, light-up scooters, and pastel chalk strewn about.

"Shit," I thought again.

Thinking my downshifted lifestyle might be coming to an end sooner rather than later, I finally called my older sister, Lety. I opened by sharing all the revelations I had found out about Mama Natalia being a curandera. But when I tried to relay every amazing detail Dora had told me, I could tell from her distracted silence and the shuffling on the phone that she was only half listening.

Lety had always been a complicated big sister. She could be super doting and protective, like when she taught me how to drive in a parking lot after my dad died. But she also had a bully side, taking out on me what my dad had taken out on her. I could see now how hard it must have been for her as the firstborn daughter, getting pushed into being a child beauty queen when she was only four years old because pretty was prized, and pretty was expected to perform.

The dirty little secret about Lety was that she was as smart as she was cute. She was also naturally *shy*. She told me once that she hated crowds, yet she was always forced in front of them, so everyone could ooh and ahh over her perfect heart-shaped face, big doe eyes, and shiny black hair. Growing up, she kept up that cheery always-on personality, though she started to rebel in her teens: smoking cigarettes, riding in fast cars, and getting into fights. My macho Mexican father tried to tame her wildness, but then he was gone, and Lety was left to figure it out on her own.

"How are you doing?" I asked.

"I'm tired all the time," she confessed. "I don't know if I can do this."

Lety had been sober for just ten months after years of using, and it must have felt like an astronaut rocketing back to Earth: dizzying and disorienting. My baby sister Paloma had gone down to Texas to visit, and she told me that Lety had been unusually quiet and uncharacteristically unsure of herself.

I understood how hard it must feel to walk this slippery slick path without being able to push your favorite escape button—I really did. I was feeling tense as hell myself and itching for a drink. I was so happy Lety was sober but terrified she would slip. I didn't know what to say or how to make it better, so I just told her that I loved her. Then I hung up, exhausted myself and freshly worried. Desperately needing some air, I left my house and walked toward a nearby trailhead that led to the river.

I was trying to burn off this simmering anxiety when my mom called me on my cell.

"What's happening, Mom?" I asked, descending a wide, gravelly path.

She sighed, and her voice sounded so heavy, I could feel the weight of it through the phone. "It's Apolonia."

My little sister Apolonia had been going through it. First it was a contentious divorce, followed by a bad car accident that left her unable to work for months. My mom had moved Apolonia and her kids in with her to help out. But each setback had taken its toll. Over the years, I tried to be there for Apolonia, feeling that protectiveness of an older sister, but it usually devolved into a fight, with her getting defensive and me feeling frustrated. My mom always came to me to vent, but it was hard to hold space without taking action.

I listened as my mom fretted about both Lety and Apolonia. A familiar dull throb began to ache in my chest. I didn't say anything, not at first. I just stopped walking and looked around at the forest. All the trees started to look the same. Finally, I said, "We can't go on like this, Mom. We need help."

This time, my mom said nothing. Instead, we both sighed, breathing in the same recycled sadness.

That night after dinner, as we sat outside watching the girls play in the yard, I talked to Lars about the job. I had gone through my first interview, and the HR person called me immediately afterward to say it went well and she'd email soon to schedule the next interview with the person who would be my boss.

"Congrats, babe!" said Lars as the girls bounced on their little trampoline.

"Yeah, thanks," I said, trying to seem excited. I knew I should be happy, that this was a great opportunity. But after I hung up with the HR person earlier, I felt a tightness in my chest and a weird tension in my neck and shoulders. I was feeling that constriction now.

Lars must have read my body language because he said, "This doesn't sound like your last job at all."

"Yeah, that's true."

"Really!" Lars continued. "I am excited for you! I think this job could be a real opportunity for you. You are so great at what you do, but at your last job, you had to put out so many fires, you were just sad and stressed all the time.

"But now," Lars continued, "you can start over with a healthy company *and* you'll get to do things differently."

Everything Lars said was true. My last job had flattened me, but this time could be different. Maybe?

A few days later, I got a text on my phone.

"Rev. Virginia Marie Rincón Curandera."

More confused than ever and desperate for some guidance, I had reached out to my cousin Patty, asking if she knew any curanderas I could study with. She immediately recommended her friend. Virginia was a curandera, an Episcopalian reverend, and a former nurse. She was also a Tejana like us, but she had just moved to Albuquerque. Patty had actually taken Apolonia and my mom to Virginia for a limpia, so Virginia knew a little of my background. She sounded perfect to me.

And when we connected via Zoom the next week, she was as wonderful as I hoped. Virginia was probably in her sixties, a grandma of two, and had short spiky hair. Calm and wise, she opened our session with a short meditation, but soon our *platica*— our heart-to-heart talk—was peppered with old-school Chicano slang words like *órale*. I loved her immediately.

Virginia asked me if I was a curandera. "Maybe?" I replied, uncertain. "I want to be," I continued, sounding even less convinced.

Then, after a long pause, I blurted out the truth. "I'm nervous to call myself a curandera," I confessed. "My great-grandmother, *she* was a curandera. It runs in my family. But right now, I just feel like a big fake, wannabe curandera. I know it's not true, but I have all these negative voices in my head. I feel like I have some sort of curandera impostor syndrome!"

"That is the voice of colonization keeping you from your medicine, comadre! Don't listen," she admonished.

She was right. Under Spanish rule, our Indigenous and African ancestors had to fight, hide, and adapt to keep practicing our medicines. Then assimilation and religion looked down at these ancient wisdom practices, deeming them old-fashioned or witchcraft. I had read that Curanderismo was illegal in my home state of Texas well into the 1970s,[1] so practitioners like Mama Natalia practiced at their own risk. So many people and institutions had tried to deny and erase this beautiful wisdom.

They had done a good job because now I didn't need anyone else to hold me back. Growing up, I had ignored and undervalued Curanderismo, and now I didn't believe in my own abilities to practice it. I was blocking myself. My self-doubt was my own colonized thinking.

"You have to stay in your Ser, in your energy field," Virginia told me.

In Spanish, *ser* means "to be," but Virginia was talking about Ser as an energy state or way of being.

"When you are in your Ser," she explained, "when you are centered and focused, you'll be clear on why you are doing what you are doing."

Virginia went on to say that Ser is our natural, un-sustoed state. "It's who you are without your ego or hurts. Ser is your essence. It's your true nature. And when you act from there, you will know what to do."

I exhaled, sensing the truth of this deeply because, to me, Ser was easier to feel than to describe. Dropping into the sacred waters of self-knowing is what Ser feels like. My Ser was that knowing feeling I'd had when I bought a one-way ticket to New York and didn't look back. My Ser whispered that I *would* be a mom even though I was getting older and had no partner in sight. And my Ser guided me out of my stressful job and onto this healing path of Curanderismo. My Ser whispered that everything would be okay, as opposed to my susto, which filled me with worry and panic.

Your Ser is your unbounded, intelligent nature, like the natural way a tree grows. We know how to move in the world, but we get stunted when something bad happens. The susto makes us forget ourselves and the pieces of us left behind in the trauma. So when we are less whole, we become more susceptible to what society and others say. "Are you sure you want to grow that way? This way is better, more successful, the right way, the way we always do it." And so we listen.

But deep down, our Ser knows. It lies below the susto, intact and untouchable, always present, always waiting. And sometimes, it catches our attention. It's usually when we are quiet: in the middle of the night, in the shower, on a run. And it's always saying the same thing: "I love you; I got you; *you know*."

"You have to stay close to your Ser," said Virginia.

"What does that mean?" I asked.

"For me," she explained, "quiet time and contemplation bring me close to my Ser."

I understood. "Hmm," I thought, considering. "I think for me, meditation and now learning Curanderismo are helping me feel . . . more rooted," I said, finding the word for how I had started to feel lately.

"That's right, comadre," she said approvingly.

"When I practice Curanderismo, doing limpia or working in the garden, I feel natural and good." As I said this, I realized it was true, like telling someone you love them for the first time. "But when I'm not present, just ruminating on the past and worrying about the future, I feel scared and unsure."

"¡Ándale!" she said. I was getting it.

Virginia and I talked about ways we get taken out of our Ser and pulled back into our sustos and susto responses—ways that we handled our trauma.

"Shit," I thought, feeling the magnitude of this land in my body.

When my dad died, I flew away because I didn't want to feel the pain his death caused me and my family. In its place, I held tight to my toughness and ability to survive. I rechanneled my hurts into ambition and recast any discomfort into my own daring. I was so proud of how hard I worked, how brave I was to run toward a life so far away from the pain of my family—a pain we were only now beginning to reckon with. But before this conversation with Virginia, I never stopped to consider that I was actually running *away* from everything. To avoid my susto, I realized, I was just hiding in the hustle. Maybe my deep pride in working myself ragged wasn't a rite of passage or a badge of honor. Maybe it was a susto response, no different from my drinking or my compulsion for getting involved in other people's dramas. And these susto responses only ever work for a little while. Eventually, they cause more stress and pain and strain everything you care most about.

"We all have many sustos throughout our lives," said Virginia. "They're like sticky notes one on top of the other," she continued, patting her chest. "But we usually have one *gran* susto—one great trauma—of our lives."

Immediately I knew what my gran susto was. "My father was in the hospital all the time after his cancer diagnosis," I began, saying aloud my most painful memory. "Family members were at his bedside almost around the clock, keeping him company and helping out if he needed anything. Usually adults or older cousins, but once I was asked to go. I remember sitting next to him as he stared blankly at the TV that was hanging from a wall, showing some game show, like *The Price Is Right*. We didn't talk. He didn't ask me about school, and I didn't ask him about dying. And after what felt like an excruciatingly long time, he finally fell asleep. I was bored and so uncomfortable, so I left his room and went to a quiet waiting area. But I still couldn't breathe. So I opened a window and crawled onto the black roof. It felt sandpapery where I sat and read the book that I'd brought with me. I don't know how long I was gone, but when I went back, my cousin Patty was there. My dad was awake and angry that I'd left him. He told my mom not to bring me back. He said I was a 'worthless sitter.'"

"It's still bothering you," Virginia said gently, noticing my watery eyes.

Choked up, I just nodded.

"What kind of cancer did your father die from?" she asked. When I told her it was pancreatic that spread to the liver, she nodded. "That is associated with anger; he was dying from *anger*."

I have always been surrounded by anger. My parents and all three sisters are fire signs, and all have fiery tempers. Growing up our house was chaotic, with lots of yelling and fighting—and sometimes hitting. I was the lone air sign, and my job, instilled early on, was not to feed that fire with my fury or feelings but instead blow in humor or goodwill—especially after my dad died. I don't think I was allowed to be angry because everyone else was. Instead, I had to be good. I remember lying in my bed years ago, after Lety and Apolonia both started to spiral, thinking, "You have to be the leader in this family. No one else is going to do it."

I don't know where that voice came from. Was it a voice of susto or Ser? Whatever it was, I took it to heart. And now I could see I had taken that need to save too far.

I had agonized over that memory at the hospital for years. Did I desert my dad in his time of need? Was I not a good helper? Did I miss the opportunity for us to have a profound talk where he shared the secrets of the universe and wisdom of how things worked?

This was the story I came back to again and again. Even after years of therapy, and even when things got better, when I did good things, shiny things, worthy things, this memory was always there like a tear in my heart. I couldn't save my dad; I couldn't save my company; and I didn't know, as much as I really wanted to, if I could save my sisters.

Trying to save everyone—that was my gran susto response.

A week later, Lucia woke up with joint aches and a fever. By lunchtime, Lars was feeling ill too, and though nothing was out of the ordinary, I started to feel creeping anxiety in my chest. This past winter had been brutally long, and it felt like my family was always sick. If it wasn't Lucia, it was Astrid, and if not Astrid, then Lars, and usually in succession. And though I knew it was probably nothing, something about the people I loved the most being sick, and at the same time, was making me feel helpless and scared.

I took Lucia to the doctor, and tests showed that she had a typical virus that Astrid had tested positive for the week before. I mentioned to the doctor that the girls seemed sick a lot, and she replied breezily with, "They're kids," and reminded me that joint pain was common with viruses. Still, after seeing my anxiety, she ordered some extra tests and sent us on our way.

At home, I took Lucia upstairs with me, and as she watched *Wild Kratts*, I realized I was having trouble catching my breath. I didn't want to freak Lucia out, and I didn't know what was happening myself, so I sat on my meditation cushion, trying to calm myself down. But as I looked out at the big Douglas fir, all I could think was, "I can't take any more. I won't survive. If something happens to anyone in my family, I'll die, and they'll need to bury me too."

It was a fucked-up thought, and thinking it scared me even more.

I kept trying to catch my breath, but I felt as though I was strapped in on a roller coaster that was zooming down, down, down, and I couldn't make it stop. I squeezed my eyes shut and whimpered. I honestly felt as if I was losing my mind. I thought of calling Virginia for a limpia, but I was paralyzed. Instead, I sat there, gripping my cushion for five minutes, quietly weeping and praying because I didn't want to scare Lucia.

Finally, I was able to move and gave myself a limpia with rosemary and an egg. I needed it all. I grabbed Lucia off the couch, much to her annoyance, handed her my phone to watch a video, and while she was occupied with a cartoon, I rubbed an egg over her body too, praying hard.

The vice grip on my heart slowly began to release. I could breathe again. It was probably the limpia, or maybe I had just worn myself out from the violence of my own neurosis. Whatever it was, I felt quieted enough to be able to take care of my family. I picked up Astrid from day care, gave Lars some medicine, and read the girls bedtime stories while I caressed their heads. As I was about to fall asleep, totally depleted, I prayed to my angels to protect us all and slipped into a deep, thoughtless slumber.

The next day, Lars and Lucia were feeling better, but they both stayed home to rest. After making sure they were good, I left them together, cozy on the couch, to take a walk.

There is a beautiful waterfall near my house, and as I walked on the trail alongside the running brook, I saw the truth as clear as the water below: susto was rearing its ugly head. My father was diagnosed with cancer when he was forty-five. Just days away from my forty-fifth birthday, I was having a total fucking meltdown.

I sat down on a rock overlooking the waterfall. I didn't know if it was the freely flowing water or the crashing sound that would conceal my cries, but in that cradle of nature, I broke down in heaving sobs. I was heartbroken that both Lety and Apolonia were still struggling after all these years. I hated that the twin afflictions of substance use disorder and susto wouldn't leave my family alone. I was pissed that Apolonia didn't have health care and couldn't get the therapy I felt she needed. And though Lety was getting better, I was bitter about a messed-up system that saw Latinas going to jail at higher rates than ever—many due to drug and mental health issues. I felt guilty for leaving my kids and my own dreams to try to save someone else's. I was angry at my dad for dying. And mostly, I was furious because I wanted so desperately to help my sisters, but I couldn't seem to make a goddamned difference no matter how hard I tried. And that made me want to scream.

In Curanderismo, rage is called *bilis*, and I was feeling that boiling fury now. Looking at the dirt under my feet, I was consumed by an idea. In one of my Curanderismo books, I read one way to relieve your anger was to go to your backyard, dig a hole, and yell all your problems into it. Then you covered it, and supposedly they were buried.

This sounded totally crazy—and exactly what I needed at that moment. Looking around to see if anyone was watching, I knelt down and began to dig a hole with my hands. It had just rained, and the dirt was soft and moist. I created a small pit and tentatively stuck my face in, smelling the clean earth. Feeling like I was about to blow, I took some deep breaths, then let it all come out. "I hate that my sisters are suffering!" I screamed. "And I hate that my mom doesn't listen to anything I say! I hate that I don't have a father! And

I hate that he died! I hate that I'm gonna die! I hate that everyone I love is going to die! I hate everythiiiiiiiiiiiiiiiiiiing!"

I wailed into the ground.

After a few sobbing breaths, I heard a noise and lifted my head out of the hole. Chest heaving, I watched a graceful deer walk slowly through the trees. And in that moment, I felt my Ser. Underneath that pent-up anger was a warmth in my belly that radiated the truth: that even in absolute pain, in soul-hurting sadness, there was something deeper in me that remained intact. A wholeness I could relax into instead of a brokenness I had to keep running from.

I began to put dirt back in the hole, burying my bilis. Then I got up, brushed myself off, and walked home.

In our bathroom, I looked in the mirror; I had dirt everywhere: on my forehead, on my cheeks, and under my chin. I was about to rub it off, but I stopped myself. I liked it. I looked like a warrior.

I walked back out into our garden, feeling wilder and freer, energized by my free-flowing anger. Looking around, I had this strong urge to pull everything up. To rip out all the roots with my bare hands, leaving just naked soil.

"Fuck the job offer," I told myself.

It was a good offer, a great one even. But not for me, not now. I was never going to gather all the pieces of myself if I kept throwing them away like crumbs to all the shiny, squawking birds who beckoned.

I needed to start following my Ser, not my susto. No more retreating. No more running. No more doubting.

I looked around at my garden. I was ready to gather my weapons. I was ready to fight.

Get Rooted Practice #3
Susto or Ser? Body Check

After my conversation with my new spiritual maestra, Virginia, I kept asking myself, What was Ser? Was it my soul? Maybe, but my soul could fly away, and my Ser never left. Was it my heart? That was the place that had been calling to me more and more. Yet, one day, my heart would stop, and my Ser would live forever. Was it my ancestors? When my Ser spoke to me, it felt like the voice of my grandmother telling me, "It's okay, mija. It's okay."

My Ser felt like God.

Not some booming voice calling from a bush but a gentle voice, calling from inside.

People have different names for this knowing voice: your higher self, your "spirit," or intuition. It matters less what we call it and more that we learn to listen to this deep wisdom.

"Am I acting from susto or Ser?" This is the question I have my clients ask themselves so we can try to determine what their Ser, or truth, really wants—and whether they are just acting out of trauma and what they think will help them avoid pain or give a temporary fix to that feeling of not-enoughness. Another way to consider it might be this: "Am I acting from my trauma or my truth?" One of my maestros, Laurencio, once said, "Susto makes you shrink." That smallness, that fear, is a sign of susto, and it's our Ser to grow fully back into ourselves.

If it's not so obvious where an impulse is coming from, try this test:

Deepen your breath, and quiet your mind. Think about a decision you are pondering, such as buying a new house or leaving your job.

Don't listen to the voices in your head. Breathe, and drop into your body. How does your body feel, expanded and free—or constricted and tight? When I pondered taking that job, my chest felt tight, and I felt a sadness in my heart, knowing that while it was such a good opportunity, it just wasn't the right fit or time for me.

Susto makes you shrink, but your Ser invites you to make space. Your body doesn't lie, so check in for clues on the things that make you shrink and the things that make you expand.

I once signed up to lead a huge project. It was a prestigious gig that paid well. But as I began working, I started experiencing insomnia, which I had never had before. For weeks I had trouble sleeping. I would wake up every night and not be able to doze back off for hours; it was horrible. Then one exhausted day, I had this crystal-clear thought: "What do you need to wake up to?" I knew what it was. I had to cancel my commitment to this beloved project. It was not the right fit and not the right time. My head kept wanting to make it work, but my body, and Ser, knew better.

It might be hard at first to know which internal voice to trust. Feel into it, and start practicing. Your Ser will get stronger—and so will your ability to spot your sustos and the clever ways you learned to deal with them, ways you no longer need.

PART TWO

The North: Time to Meet the Family

4

Setting Your Table

Dear Dad,

It's been a while since we last spoke. But I really miss you, and I need your help. Lety is doing so much better, thank goodness, after so many years. But I need you to help make sure she stays on track! Paloma is really good. You'd be super proud; she's tough and funny and kind of bratty. But we all put up with her 'cause underneath, she is the most sensitive and is tender on the inside, like a crab. I am worried about Apolonia, though. She's been lost for a while. Can you help her find her way back?

I've been doing our family tree and read that we are from a state in northern Mexico called Coahuila, which was once joined with Tejas, so we've been in this region for generations. The Indigenous people from the area are called Coahuiltecans, which means to be "among the trees." Isn't that beautiful?

I remember visiting that area when we were little. We ate in a restaurant that had a cooked goat on a spit displayed in the window, and I thought it was the most horrible thing ever, and then you ordered the cabrito for lunch, and I started crying! Do you remember? Did you know Coahuila is also the birthplace of nachos? Pretty cool, I know.

Please come visit me, in my dreams and meditations, and keep sending me signs. I promise to listen. I miss you!

Te amo,
Robyn

After spending nearly two months in the east moving winds, doing limpia, and trying to distinguish between my susto and Ser, it was time to change directions. I had learned to call the directions in the order of east, west, north, and then south, so the west should come next.

But the north was calling. It's the direction of ancestors and the place from which we call in our ancestral guides to be with us and protect us. And, honestly, I needed them now more than ever. Even though I felt better and rooted after releasing so much pent-up bilis yelling into the dirt that day, the gripping anxiety attack I had when Lucia and Lars got sick along with almost abandoning myself for a job and a life I knew wouldn't help me get rooted showed me that my fears were still flexing hard-core.

Trusting my newly found Ser, I pivoted to the north. To honor this new direction, I decided to redo my altar. I had started with a small makeshift one, but it was time for an upgrade. I swept and cleared the space, giving it a good limpia, moving in the winds of calm and connection and moving out anger and doubts. I had read that another name for an altar in Spanish is a *mesa*. So I pushed together two wooden cubes and covered them with a colorful Mexican rebozo.

Now I was ready to invite my ancestors to the table. I set up photos of my father alongside my grandparents. I also placed a beautiful old photo of my grandmother sitting on my great-great-grandmother's lap. And as the centerpiece there was Mama Natalia. As offerings, I plucked some marigolds and placed them next to my tall botanica candle of La Virgen. This all felt very Día de los Muertos, but why couldn't I connect with my ancestors all year long?

I finished by placing objects to symbolize the four elements: a shimmery turkey feather I had found, spiral shells from the beach in Mexico, a big chunk of amethyst a dear friend had given me to break bad habits (and help me stay away from alcohol), and a *sahumerio*[1] (clay incense burner). As I sat in front of my newly set table to meditate, I couldn't help but think back to the last time I connected with my ancestors.

It was six years ago, when I first found out I was pregnant with Lucia. Lars and I had only been dating for three months, so we were surprised as heck to be pregnant but thrilled just the same. We had both wanted kids after each going through long relationships that didn't pan out, and I had been longing for a baby, a girl particularly.

A few years before I had even met Lars, I was traveling in Mexico and saw a tiny embroidered sundress that I fell in love with. I bought it and hung it in the back of my closet for years. It traveled with me after breakups, to different cities, and finally to a house all my own as I continued to imagine the day I could put it on my own daughter.

So to be unexpectedly pregnant with a man I already knew I loved—and firmly in my late thirties—felt like a miracle. But our excitement was curtailed when I started spotting blood a few days after finding out about the pregnancy. Terrified, I called my dear friend Evelyn, who had suffered a miscarriage. She told me to go to the hospital right away.

As I sat in the emergency room, I prayed as I had not prayed in a long time, getting down on my knees in that cold, clinical examining room. "God, Dad, angels, whoever is out there, please, *please* make this baby safe!" I begged.

Through a sonogram, the doctor saw a beating heart; the baby was fine. I burst into tears of relief. But he continued to say that he didn't know why I was bleeding and warned I could still lose the baby, so I should be on bed rest for the duration of my first trimester.

Relieved but equally terrified, I laid low and began to pray and meditate with a vengeance. Every morning, I'd sit on my blue meditation cushion, place my hands on my belly, and send my mama love and protective energy to my growing baby. I had just completed a yearlong yoga and meditation training, and instinctively I began to practice a visual meditation where you call on a guide to help you. In my mind, I called out naturally to my dad, but just like my Mexican family, all of my relatives who had passed showed up! It was amazing to see them again: my mom's parents and my dad's mom and my stepbrother—I could picture them perfectly. They were all hugging me and crowding around me, so excited to see me, like a heavenly reunion. My dear friends Danny, Rhonda, and Kenny, who had passed away far too young, were also there. The guest of honor, though, was my dad.

I hadn't dreamed about him in years, but now I could see him clearly: healthy and wearing a white guayabera. For some reason, we were all on a beach, and we sat in a circle and prayed together on the soft sand for the health and protection of my unborn child. At the end of our prayer, hands still clasped, my dad looked at me and said, "She's going to be fine." I felt a deep peace and calm, until my eyes flew open when I registered what he had said.

"She!"

Though Lars and I didn't officially know the sex of our baby until many weeks after, I already knew she would be a girl. My dad told me.

All throughout my pregnancy, I was able to drop into meditation and visit with my family. Sometimes it was just my dad, and sometimes I sat with my grandparents in the shade on that imagined beach. But throughout that pregnancy, and Astrid's too, I felt close to my relatives who had transitioned. I enjoyed seeing them in my meditations, and I talked to them in my real life, as if they were there listening. I said hello when a song came on that reminded me of them. And I laughed when they showed me so many obvious signs that they were there: numbered sequences on the clock and phone, butterflies that flew so close to me I could see their intricate patterns. Once I laughed out loud after being hurried and flustered in an elevator when my eye stopped on a button that read, "Help is on the way." I began to understand then that our ancestors are always with us.

I had spoken to other people who had similar experiences connecting with ancestors during pregnancy. We all agreed that there was something about bringing life that created a portal to another world. But once my life got filled with kids and work, I got too busy, and they faded into the background. Now I was ready to reconnect. And in a way, I felt pregnant again. I was growing something, birthing my own evolution, and I yearned to connect with my ancestors again.

The ancient Mexica believed that death was just another realm of life. They believed not only that we can commune with spirits but that they can, in fact, come back to earth and aid us, whether through dreams or visions or in a form, like a hummingbird. That is why they have celebrated a form of Día de los Muertos since before Columbus even touched this continent.

They used the scent of copal—an aromatic tree resin—to connect with the ancestors. To light copal is a little elaborate. You first need a base to burn it in, like a ceramic plate or a sahumerio. Then, you make a little fire or ignite a small charcoal tablet, which is what I had. And when that starts to get nice and hot, you drop small pieces of the copal resin on top, which emit that heavenly, woodsy scent.

I was trying to light copal now at my altar, and it was not working. I had tried lighting the charcoal tablet, but I couldn't tell if it was lit or not. "Ouch!" I yelled when I gave it a tap to test it. Yup, it was lit. Next, I tore off a chunk of copal, which was crazy sticky, so I had trouble getting it off my hands and onto the tablet. Finally, I just flung it into the sahumerio, and it missed the charcoal, landing on the side, where it melted sadly, no elaborate plumes of smoke rising. "Damn it!" I yelled out, frustrated not only by my novice abilities but also because I wanted some divine connection and comfort *now*.

Abandoning this sacrilege, I decided to light a copal incense stick. "Okay, this I can handle," I said aloud. Once that was nicely smoking, I exhaled and tried the same meditation I had used to call in my ancestors before. After a few minutes, I began to visualize myself on that familiar beach, but I had trouble staying with the vision. I was mentally distracted and kept getting pulled away with thoughts of my kids and all the things I had to do. Ughhh. I was clearly out of practice. I made myself sit there for about twenty minutes. I didn't get any visions or messages, but I did feel calmer.

With my eyes now open, I began looking at the photos of my father. One was a black-and-white picture of him with big ears and teeth, holding his high school diploma and looking too skinny for his suit. Another photo of my dad was taken at a business fund raiser, the year before he was diagnosed. Sporting a tux, he looked handsome and stout, the embodiment of success. The last picture was taken just two months before he died. It showed just his profile, and his cheekbones protruded. He was bundled up in a lumberjack jacket, scarf, and newsboy cap. His hand was resting on his chin, as if he were pondering something, a secret or some grand wisdom I couldn't yet grasp.

I didn't know much about my dad's life before fatherhood. Most of my favorite memories with him are swimming in the river, playing in the park, and driving through the desert on our family road trips. I had inherited my dad's love of nature, and I felt the most at home, closest to my Ser, near water and trees and mountains. My dad grew up in a one-bedroom home with his five siblings and parents. His front porch and backyard served as extra bedrooms. No wonder he felt so comfortable under the stars and sky. But what was *his* nature like?

Wanting to know more, I emailed one of my dad's younger sisters, Paola, for help.

"Your dad was a natural leader who was always very popular . . . All the girls loved him . . . He liked cereal so much we nicknamed him 'Indio Cheerio.' He was a natural handyman and self-taught photographer . . . His daughters were his life."

About us girls, Paola wrote that my dad was the hardest on Lety because she was the oldest. Lety was rebellious, and he was a demanding father, pushing her to succeed, enrolling her in chess classes and tae kwon do. Apparently, he thought I was the smartest (probably because I always had my head in a book), and I remember us reading the paper together and him quizzing me to prep for my spelling bee.

About Apolonia, Paola wrote that he loved her wild energy and never tried to curb it. My dad always babied Paloma, but, tragically, it was those two who had the least amount of time together.

I asked her what my dad thought about his illness. Was he sad, heartbroken, worried? She replied that he kept his thoughts to himself, though he often had a faraway and sad expression. I thought of the photo on my altar where he looked thin, with his fingers pensively resting on his chin.

I recalled a Mexica poem.

Not forever on earth, only a little while here.
Though it be jade it falls apart, though it be gold it wears away,
though it be quetzal plumage it is torn asunder.
Not forever on earth, only a little while here.[2]

My dad understood all too well that only a little while are we here.

To go deeper in learning about my father and family, I spent days and weeks researching my genealogy and found a ton on Ancestry. com about my dad. It was amazing and strange, like the virtual version of creeping into someone's attic to go through old boxes of photos and papers.

I learned that my father graduated from college in 1969 with a degree in government. He was into the Chicano movement and La Raza Unida and took my mom to see the activist Cesar Chavez when he came to Texas for a farmworkers' rally. I once interviewed Dolores Huerta, who championed farmworkers' rights alongside Cesar Chavez and coined the famous phrase "¡Sí, se puede!" Dolores gave me a treasured piece of advice. "Know your history," she told me. "Know where you came from."

My quest to know my history took a sad turn when I came across my uncle Oscar's death certificate. Oscar was my dad's older, and only, brother and died when he was just seventeen, killed at a party that my grandmother tried to talk him out of going to. It listed his cause of death as a massive hemorrhage from a bullet wound inflicted by a .32-caliber pistol.

The family story was that it was an accident. Kids playing with guns. But a newspaper article I found from 1955 reported my father's older brother died "after a bullet struck him in the heart during a scramble for the weapon." A "scramble for the weapon" didn't sound like an accident. I had known of this tragedy growing up, but seeing it in black-and-white brought tears to my eyes.

A photo I found of Oscar showed a lanky, handsome young man with big brown eyes and big ears just like my dad's. How cool would it have been to grow up knowing this Tío Oscar? From what I heard, he was sweet and relaxed. Paola told me that my father and Oscar were the closest of the six children because they were only two years apart and the only brothers. My dad was the outgoing one, and Oscar was shyer. I had never heard my dad talk about his brother, not once. But the susto of his brother's death must have lived with him.

My own siblings' sustos were activated when a call to my mom to share what I had learned about my father quickly turned into more worry about my sisters. My mom was so relieved that Lety was doing better, but she still complained that Lety didn't call her enough.

While we were talking, I could hear Apolonia yelling at someone in the background. "Is everything okay?" I asked, uncertain of what was happening.

"Everything's okay," my mom said quickly, trying to get back to our conversation.

"Apolonia doesn't sound okay," I said, pushing back.

"She's fine. You don't live with her, I do!" she responded. She was letting me know this was the end of the conversation.

It was true. I wasn't close by to see what was happening. So I just let it go.

Still, I didn't always trust my mom to tell me the truth about struggles that were happening in her life. Maybe she wanted to shield me, or maybe tragedy had taught her to tie up your heart and carry on. But that constant plowing through pain was dangerous, because your tolerance becomes too high. Since my dad's death, we had endured a series of hardships, and I felt like we had lost our family baseline for what was normal or healthy. I remember once when Paloma and I traveled home for Christmas, and Lety offered to host Christmas Eve dinner. It had been a while since we'd seen her, and we were all excited to be together. But when we arrived, nothing was ready. The house was dark, there was no food set out, and Lety looked anxious and surprised to see us when she finally answered the door. She rushed out of the house to go to the "grocery store" and never came back. Instead, my mom, Paloma, and I sat at the empty dinner table, all dressed up in our holiday clothes, just waiting. My mom sunk in her chair, looking little and lost, as Paloma cursed angrily, furious she had wasted her time visiting a family that constantly disappointed, while I couldn't open the bottle of cabernet I had brought fast enough, gulping wine and trying to calm the shock of witnessing how far Lety's substance use had taken her. Paloma and I stopped going home for the holidays after that. When I told my mom the truth of why we didn't want to go home anymore, she acted like I was exaggerating. That gaslighting destabilized me, and I wondered, "How are they not seeing how fucked up this all is? Am I the crazy one? Can't they see everything is on fire?"

Later, at dinner, Lars poured himself some wine, and I poured myself some too. I hadn't had a drop of alcohol in the months since I started this journey, and I felt lightheaded almost immediately. When I poured a generous second glass, he gave me a look, and I gave him a defiant look right back. Lars didn't love my drinking. Specifically, he didn't love my moody hangovers or having to pay more for our car insurance when I got a DUI several years back. I put the glass to my lips and drank, feeling the familiar release radiate through my body. I knew that I was breaking my own promise to stay sober during these 260 days. But I was just so fucking sick of everything. I needed a break—to be gone, floating above it all.

I didn't take a third glass, but my head was foggy and hurting the next morning, and I had a sour taste in my mouth, filled with the regret of betraying my own Ser.

My dad was a drinker who liked beer and bourbon. He was a loving dad, but he had a cutting mean streak too. Looking back, I almost felt like I had two dads—one tender and one harsh—and I never knew which one I would get. I didn't want to be like that. But if I wanted something different, I would have to do something different. I would have to be someone different. And only two months into my healing, I just didn't know how.

I needed my Yoda.

"You need to spend time with the ancestors, comadre," Virginia admonished me after I told her about my stressful conversation with my mom and fitful memories. I explained to Virginia that I had been setting my alarm daily for fifteen to twenty minutes, trying to dive-bomb my way into sacred connection with my ancestors. "Talk to them, in front of your altar, yes, but when you smell *las flores*, say, 'Thank you, abuelos.' When you cook, say, 'Thank you, abuelos, for the recipe.' When you play music, dance with them in your kitchen! Don't just pick up the phone when you need something! You are in relationship with los abuelos. Talk to them, pray to them, offer them *regalitos*. Then listen, mija, listen *here*," she said, touching her heart. "When you don't listen to your own heart, you are disrespecting the ancestors! Slow down and take the time, mija!"

Virginia was right, as usual.

Now that I had paused from my "go, go, go" lifestyle, I could finally hear my Ser speaking to me. It was telling me to turn around. I needed to look back before I could go forward. The soul pieces I had to retrieve were not only in my past, but intertwined in the lives and stories of my family's past. To truly understand myself, I needed to know my dad, my grandparents, and the ancestors who were trying to speak to me from these photos. What were their hopes and dreams? Their triumphs and regrets? Their songs and sustos? And how could that help us now? I once read that the length of a tree's roots is equal to its height. Was I able to soar not only because of my own ambitions and resilience but because of the strength and perseverance of all those who came before? And if

I was feeling stunted or impeded, was it all on me? Or was there an ancestral block or decay I needed to repair or remove? Was there a door I could unlock, a path I could clear so my sisters, my mom, and I could finally get rooted and flourish? With each relative I unearthed, each story uncovered, I was inviting my ancestors back to the table, feasting on the memories, and nourishing myself in the rich dishes of our old ways. Sitting with them, listening, learning, linking the past to the future is how I was finding my place.

When I hung up with Virginia, I sat down on the floor in front of my altar, moving aside my meditation cushion and stretching out on the floor. I put on a Chicano oldies song my parents loved, "Lo Mucho Que Te Quiero" by René y René, and I tried again to light the finicky copal. This time, I slowly let the charcoal tablet burn, and when I saw the red embers flickering, I added small pieces of copal on top, ever so carefully. Soon, white plumes began to waft up with that sweet, woodsy scent that felt like church to me. Warmer than the Catholic masses of my childhood, it was the holiness of the forests, the ministry of nature. Listening to the music, I felt transported back to the living room of my childhood with my parents and grandparents laughing and dancing. Inhaling that scent, I knew my ancestors were here; they had always been here. I didn't have to do anything. Connection wasn't something we forced but rather something natural we let happen when we slowed way the fuck down, put on some good music, and just let ourselves *be*.

I had been going about it all wrong in my demanding modern way—wanting the connection *now*. I'd been coming at my ancestors, instead of being with my ancestors, demanding life-changing advice. But that's not how life-changing advice is given, is it? It never stands on the mountaintop proclaiming, "Hey, listen up, here's the secret to life that's gonna make it all make sense!" Instead, it's quiet knowledge passed while doing your homework, stories shared in the car while running errands, words of encouragement given when you fall on your ass. I'd been looking for the big reveal, but maybe it's never that movie-like. Instead, it's whispered in the wind, it rises from the pot of beans, it's in listening to music your parents fell in love to. Looking at that pensive image of my dad, I realized he taught me so much when we were together that I was still just awakening to. And as painful as it was, he taught me even more in those gaps when I thought I had to figure it out alone. As unsure as I was feeling right now walking this slippery slick road, I did not feel alone. I laid on my back, enveloped in music and smoke and memory, letting myself be held by the arms of mis abuelas.

Wanting to hear more about Mama Natalia, I made another phone date with my great-aunt Dora and called her while I took a walk. I knew how lucky I was to have this ninety-two-year-old treasure chest to share stories of our family, and I knew in my heart and Ser that as strong and healthy as she was, Dora wouldn't be around forever. Curious about Mama Natalia's gifts as a tarot card reader, I asked Dora if she thought Mama Natalia was a psychic, and she said, "Yes, mija, she was an *espiritualista*.* She knew. Mama Natalia would tell us, 'Get ready, someone's coming!' and sure enough, someone would show up at the house."

Dora continued. "I remember this one day. Mama Natalia was in the kitchen cooking when she stopped and had this funny look on her face. She told me, 'I'm tired, mija. I'm gonna go lie down.' I was about fourteen years old at the time," Dora explained. "Then, a few minutes later, I heard a man's voice say, 'Can you bring me some water?' Well, there was no man in the house," continued Dora, "so I didn't know who it was! I went into Mama Natalia's room, and the voice was coming from her! It was the voice of my grandfather, Papa Julio, who had just passed away. He told me, 'Put the glass of water on the table, mija, and go get your mama.' I ran

---

* An espiritualista is a type of curandera who makes connections between the earth and the spiritual realm. There are different types of curanderxs, each with their own specialty. Some include a *partera*, who is a midwife; a *sobadora*, who is a bodyworker; a *hierbero*, who is a healer who has great knowledge of herbal medicine; a *consejera*, who is like a counselor or therapist; a *huesero*, who is a bonesetter, akin to a modern-day chiropractor; a *santera*, who works with the Santería religion to heal; and a *temazcalera*, who leads temazcal ceremonies.

and got Mom, and we stayed talking to Papa Julio for about thirty minutes. He came back because he was worried about Mama Natalia and us and wanted to make sure we were okay. Finally, he said, 'Take care of Mama Natalia. She has a lot on her shoulders now.' And then he left. When I looked over at the bedside table, the glass of water I had brought in was almost half empty.

"I remember it, mija, like it was today," said Dora as I listened, rapt. "A lot of people don't believe in these things. But when you see it happen, you can't stop believing."

I was floored. When I pictured Mama Natalia doing her "thing," I imagined an old lady with a cigarette in her mouth reading tarot cards and rubbing an egg over people. But if this story was to be believed, this was some next-level shit.

But one thing Mama Natalia never did, Dora warned me, was "to read the cards to her own family. She didn't want to know what was going to happen."

"How did she learn to read cards?" I asked Dora, still astonished.

"Well, mija, I think she taught herself, though her mother had the gift too. When Mama Natalia's mother, your great-great-grandmother Julianita, was about twenty-four years old, she became very sick and was actually pronounced dead," said Dora, telling another spooky story. They laid Julianita out in the living room, as was custom in the old days, surrounded by candles and covered with a veil. For about ten hours, people came to visit and pay their respects, until someone noticed stirring coming from the table. "The veil is moving!" someone exclaimed, and right at that moment, Julianita sat up and looked out onto her horrified audience.

"People started running and screaming!" said Dora. "But it was true. Julianita was indeed alive!"

After I hung up on what was our juiciest convo yet, I was still amazed. As wild as it sounded, I believed Dora.

Spending all this time sitting with my ancestors, I believed, like the Mexica did, in an afterlife: the place they wrote about in poems, "where death does not exist."

Walking along the river, I stopped and looked at the sheet of cotton-ball clouds that dotted the endless blue sky. In the distance, I saw verdant mountains and one lovely little sailboat in the river so perfectly positioned, it looked like a set designer plopped it in as the perfect final accessory. I thought about my ancestors residing where death does not exist, and in that moment, I felt that place here.

"You have to ask Tía Ximena about your dad's dream the night before he passed," wrote Aunt Paola via email. I called Aunt Ximena, my father's oldest sister, and when she answered, I asked her if my dad had shared any visions before he died.

She told me that one day, right before he passed, Ximena had walked into his hospital room and he had his hands raised up in front of him and was saying, "Can you see it? Can you see them?"

"He was looking at heaven," said my aunt. "He said he could see where we were all going to go, and he was so excited, he couldn't wait to tell your mom."

Is that what my dad was looking at as I stared at his photo in front of my altar? The place where death does not exist?

Wanting my dad close and near, I had started a journal I labeled "Daddy," and in it I wrote poetry, what the Mexica called "flower songs." I wrote letters to him, wherever he was, and felt him close and near as I told him about his granddaughters and shared frustrations about my sisters and mom. I wrote about funny and mundane things. And I wrote about things I remembered, like the time on Valentine's Day when my mom gave him a giant Hershey's Kiss, and he knew I had sneakily bitten into it because my buckteeth left two trails in the chocolate, and instead of getting mad, we just laughed and laughed.

Writing to my father felt like a conjuring. I could imagine him listening and reading, and I felt as though I were writing him back into existence, even for a little while. And then one day, I heard it, his voice in my head—that sweet sound of no other I hadn't heard in decades—and it woke up my soul. He was laughing.

I began to feel the magic of the north, that our ancestors—the ones we know, the ones we never met, and the ones we choose—not only surround us but live *in* us. Their dreams and strengths inhabit our cells, and they can hold us, carry us, and push us when we think we can no longer go on. And here in the north, as I was worried about my sisters and how this would all turn out, the spirit of our ancestors told me to trust. To fall back into the ancient waters where they were waiting all along to help me carry these burdens.

Writing down these memories, talking with Dora and my aunts, and combing through the ancestral vaults, I was bringing to life the faded outlines I had of my father and the family members I knew and the ones I still hoped to find. And in that way, I was collecting more than just clues or memories; I was gathering myself.

Get Rooted Practice #4

Write a Letter to the Ancestors

Remembering the ancestors is a form of soul retrieval. In front of our altar, we open the dialogue with our abuelos by writing a letter. Grab a pen and paper, and start writing to your ancestors. What do you want to thank them for? What do you want to ask of them? What do you want to let them know?

In the faces of my ancestors and the lines traced back were my Indigenous, Black, and European heritage. This blending of people was like Curanderismo itself, a sometimes hidden but persevering *medicina* woven into a braid of beliefs from the Old World and New. I wrote a letter to Mama Natalia to thank her for carrying on the medicina and to my Black and Indigenous ancestors who fought and hid and stirred together the pot of Curanderismo to create a healing recipe to help cure the wounds of the past and present.

By writing to our ancestors, we open the channel. We can ask them to visit us, to guide us, to share their wisdom, and to remind us that we carry the wisdom ourselves. And by praying for and listening to ancestral wisdom, we begin to strengthen our intuition and follow our Ser.

I understand not everyone might know their ancestors or have good relations with them. If the word *ancestors* isn't connecting for you, know that ancestors can work for adoptive family, stepfamily, teachers, caregivers, close friends, spiritual teachers, and people who have inspired you, like artists, musicians, and writers. Ancestors can be anyone who has helped you on your path. Like family, ancestors can be chosen.

Get Rooted Practice #5
Call in the Ancestors Meditation

This is a short and sweet meditation I use to call in and connect with my ancestors. You can record yourself reading this and play it back or find it on my website (www.robynmoreno.com/meditation).

Sit in front of your altar. Get comfortable and begin to deepen your breathing. Slowly and evenly, inhale and exhale, focusing on your breath for a few minutes to calm your mind and drop into your body.

Now close your eyes and visualize yourself in the most beautiful location you can imagine: on the beach, deep in the forest, on the moon. Really see yourself in that place, feeling happy and peaceful. You are happy to be there because this is where you'll see your ancestors. Feel the joy in your heart, and from this delight call out to your ancestor(s), "Dad! Tía! Abuelo!" Imagine them walking toward you. See them clearly in your mind's eye as they approach you, smiling. Embrace them! Laugh at the bliss of being together! Sit down, and as you look at their faces, remember all their exceptional qualities: their goodness, their selflessness, their kindness. All the things they taught you.

Give them the gifts and offerings you brought them—items they loved, like chocolates and flowers or tequila. See them smile!

Now, let them know why you are here. Ask them to help you, to stay with you, to guide you. Ask them for any message they may have for you.

Listen openheartedly as they share with you what you need to know. When you feel it's time to go, thank them. Ask them to stay with you, and let them know you are ready to receive their messages. Those could be white butterflies, a repeated sequence of numbers on a clock, like 11:11 or 4:44, their favorite song on the radio. Be receptive to the messages of the ancestors and see what you "pick up."

As you leave, give them a hug, and feel their love embrace you.

5

Becoming Remothered

"How is it?" I asked expectantly. I had just made homemade *arroz con verduras*—a recipe I learned from my friend Lupe—and was trying it out on my panel of judges: Lars, Lucia, and Astrid.

"Too much garlic," said Lars after taking a bite.

"I don't like this wice!" yelled Astrid. "I don't wike peas!" she screamed, pushing the rice off her plate.

Yikes!

I looked hopefully at Lucia. At six, she was old enough to have empathy, and I could usually count on her for culinary support. But not today. She wouldn't even take a bite. She just sniffed her fork, put it down, and reached for another quesadilla.

Ouch.

I took a bite myself . . . and it wasn't good. Lars was right. The taste of garlic overwhelmed, followed by a weird acidy aftertaste, most likely from the tomatoes. And it definitely needed more salt. Damn! This was essentially just rice and vegetables. How could I mess this up?

"I'm a terrible cook!" I wailed to Lars, totally frustrated. I'd just spent fifty dollars and nearly two hours on this *mierda*! "The only thing I can make is quesadillas!" I said, mad at myself. It was true. And technically, you don't really cook them, you just melt them.

"I like your veggie burgers," said Lars, trying to be helpful.

"Great! I can make two things!" I replied, flopping a plain corn tortilla down on my plate. I didn't want my weird rice dish either.

"Start small," said Lars encouragingly, waving a corn chip at me. "Try this recipe again and again till you've perfected it, then add on."

Lars was right, but I still wanted to dump this garlicky, clumpy mess over his head. Instead, I stood up from the table, grabbed the pan of rejected arroz, and said to Lars defeatedly, "I may just have to accept that I'm a horrible cook."

"If you are a horrible cook, *I'm* the one who's going to have to accept it," said Lars sadly as he looked down at his plate.

After weeks of researching ancestry and mentally traveling back in time learning about my dad and other long-lost relatives, I was now ready to bring their spirit forward by heading into the kitchen and reclaiming the ancestral gift of cooking.

Some of the strongest memories I had of Mama Natalia were of her in the kitchen, yet I sorely lacked my own kitchen confidence.

I inherited my lackluster cooking from my mom, who was also inconsistent in the kitchen. She did have some winning dishes, like her juicy picadillo tacos, but other meals were questionable, like her mystery meat concoctions. My sisters and I would pick up the rubbery pieces with our fork and wonder, "Is it pork? Is it steak? Is it edible?" The answer was . . . just barely.

After my dad died and my mom was overwhelmed taking care of us and trying to stay afloat financially, she gave up all pretense of trying to cook, and we found solace in takeout and Top Ramen noodles.

When I called my mom the day after the rice fiasco, demanding to know why I was cursed with no kitchen skills, she blamed it all on her mother. "My mother never taught me how to cook!" she replied. "She always kicked us out of the kitchen!"

"Did anyone teach *her* how to cook?" I asked, trying to get to the root of this culinary curse.

"No, she didn't have a mom, and her dad always dumped her with his sisters or whoever could watch her. I don't think she ever cooked until she married my father."

My mother's mother was orphaned as a child. After she was abandoned by her mother as a baby, her dad went on to remarry, randomly coming in and out of her life. As she grew up, bouncing around the homes of extended family, it seemed that Refugia—or Cookie, as she was called—only learned how to cook on the job as a young wife, and it was staunchly viewed as a necessity, not a passion. So as soon as her four daughters were out the door, she closed up her kitchen, never to cook again. Literally.

Cookie didn't know how to drive, so her noncooking forced my grandfather to take her out to eat, getting her away from the confines of her house and into the world. While I always thought that was pretty badass of her, the consequence was that I never grew up in her warm kitchen, hand-making tortillas the way you saw in commercials. Instead, to me, my grandmother was restaurants: little taco houses, where I ate a fluffy, oozing bean-and-cheese taco while staring at the black-velvet paintings of Mexica warriors that hung on the wall; or her favorite, Mi Tierra, a bustling twenty-four-hour diner that had strolling mariachis, a stretching display case of pan dulce, and rows and rows of vibrant *papel picado* hanging from the ceilings.

In these settings, my grandmother held court. She knew all the waiters by heart, and this was where she would introduce me in Spanish as her *pocha* granddaughter, using a term for Mexican Americans who don't speak Spanish. When I looked up the root of the word, I found this: the word derives from the Spanish word *pocho*, used to describe fruit that has become rotten or discolored. According to mi abuela, I had lost my flavor. And I was determined to get it back.

My dad's mom, Carlotta, was a much better cook, and her arroz con pollo, particularly her rice, is the stuff of legends. That's what I was attempting to make for my own family—except a vegan version with veggies instead of poultry. But I never asked Grandma Carlotta to teach me how to cook, a mistake I deeply regret and one I was hoping to rectify by taking cooking classes with my friend Lupe, who owned the only Mexican restaurant in my town.

Walking into Lupe's was like walking into the kitchen of the aunt or grandmother I wished lived nearby. When she first opened, I went there not only for the comfort food but for their company. Now, Lupe and her daughter, Yesenia, had become mis comadres, my homegirls. They were two of the few other Latinas in our town, and I craved both their food and their friendship.

I walked in through the back door and immediately greeted everyone in my pocha Spanish. "*Hola, cómo estás!*" I kissed Lupe, then grabbed my *mandil* from the hook, slid it over my head, tied it, and reached into a box for a small cellophane packet that contained my hairnet. I was ready for my assignment.

"Today we are making *chileatole!*" said Lupe. "And spicy green beans!"

Atole is a type of cornmeal beverage that was consumed commonly, even daily, in Mesoamerica. Atoles can be sweet or savory, and chileatole is a soup version made with corn masa, corn kernels, spinach, and peppers. Some people add meat or chicken, but today our version was vegetarian.

I had just switched from being a vegetarian to a vegan, which was not helping my cooking. I had been a vegetarian off and on for years but had recently stopped eating dairy. Though Lupe didn't really understand my plant-based diet, sometimes she indulged me and tried to plantify her traditional dishes. Other times she didn't, and I was tasked to shred chicken or stuff ground beef into poblano peppers, which I was totally fine with.

Luis Miguel was crooning on the radio while Olivia, Lupe's sous chef, showed me how to blend a soup base of masa and spinach and water.

Lupe liked a little heat in her soups—that's my girl!—so we chopped up some serrano pepper and tossed it in the blender. Now we were cooking! Then we added a sprig of epazote, which is a dried herb that smells like a mint leaf dunked in gasoline. It's most often used with beans because the legumes can stand up to the pungent quality of the herb and because epazote fights gas—the struggle is real.

Lupe was loco for epazote; it was her secret ingredient. It grows like a weed in the Americas and has long been used in cooking and medicine. In Nahuatl, the word means "skunk odor"[1] because of its strong aroma, so a little epazote goes a long way in cooking.

As I cut pieces of corn to boil in the soup, we got on the topic of how hard it was to raise children. The memory of my children rejecting my cooking was still fresh in my mind, and I shared it with the kitchen.

"I don't know how you raised five, Lupe!" I said in genuine admiration. "I can barely handle my two!"

"I always babied my kids," said Lupe. "I had five kids, and I would make five different meals for them. We do everything for our children."

She then got quiet and said, "I remember we were in an earthquake in Mexico City in 1985. It was bad. Carlos, my husband, was at work, and I was alone with the kids. I had all the kids standing underneath a door frame, and they were all screaming, 'We're gonna die, Mama!' and I said, 'No, we are not!' and we didn't."

We both had tears in our eyes. "We lost everything during the earthquake. Our apartment, our jobs. Carlos had family in New York, and he wanted to move. We were able to get visas for us and our baby, but we had to leave our four girls with Carlos's family.

"I was a teacher in Mexico City," she continued, "but when I came to the US, I was a nanny. For two years, I took care of other people's kids while mine were back in Mexico. Every single morning when I took the train to work, I was thinking of my girls. 'Do they need breakfast? Do they need help getting dressed? I should be there with them!' When we would talk to them on the phone, I would tell them, 'When you take a shower, mija, I am the warm water caressing your skin. When you feel the breeze on your way to school, that's me telling you that I love you.' I finally told Carlos, 'I can't take it. Bring me my kids, or I'm going home!' Finally, we brought them here."

I talked to Yesenia about this, and she remembered growing up in bustling Mexico City but then having to go live with their grandparents in a small town outside of Puebla for two years until they could finally send for them. Little Yesenia was only eight at the time.

"We definitely have susto, my older sister in particular, from being away from my parents for so long," Yesenia told me.

"Here, mija, enjoy this," said Lupe, handing me a bowl of the chileatole we just made.

I went out to the front of the small restaurant and sat at one of the six tables, hairnet still on, to eat. A spicy smell wafted up, and I ladled a spoonful of savory corn to my mouth. "Mmmm." I didn't know if it was because I was starving or because I was proud that I helped make this, but it was the best soup I had ever tasted. It was hearty, salty, and just plain delicious. As I slowly spooned every nourishing mouthful, the warmth and weight of the chileatole felt like a salve, gently soothing the cracks in my heart. And as I savored the subtle strength of the epazote, this resilient, formidable, and healing herb, I thought of mis comadres, Lupe and Yesenia. I ate every drop. It tasted like home.

Feeling fortified, I headed home to ask my mom for her *borracho* beans recipe. If there was one thing my mom could make, it was frijoles. Turns out hers contained beer and bacon.

Eager to make it my own, I turned back to my project and began searching online for "vegan Mexican cookbooks." One called *Decolonize Your Diet* caught my eye, and its first page included a quote from Indigenous activist Winona LaDuke: "The recovery of the people is tied to the recovery of food, since food itself is medicine, not only for the body, but for the soul, and for the spiritual connection."

Once, while visiting New Mexico, I met an amazing Chicana who owned a catering company. In addition to a cooking lesson, she gave us a lecture on food politics, reclamation, and healing. She talked about what our grandparents had to give up in terms of food and medicine to get their "white" privileges.

"What did your grandmother give up because she didn't want everyone to know you were Mexican?" she asked us. That laundry list was long: names for one. My grandmother had gone from Carmen Maria de Refugia to Cuca (which is the nickname for Refugia) to the more easily pronounceable Cookie. And Mama Natalia hid her Curanderismo talents so well we had almost lost them. Each generation seemed to know less and less: recipes lost, forgotten, or disregarded. Until you end up like me: not knowing your dishes, dialect, or yourself. The instructor called this *desmadre*. In Spanish, it meant "chaos," but it's a state of dis-mothering.

So how do we find our way?

The seeds hold the answers, she told us. Our ancestors cultivated their plants and crops with us in mind, she said. "So if we cultivate these seeds, we'll remember. *¡Chale!* Hell yeah! Find some seeds, and start growing and asking. They remember. All your songs, all your prayers, all your grandmas and grandpas—they are in those seeds." This is what *Decolonize Your Diet* was about. Reclaiming. Remembering. I ordered the book, and when it arrived, I read it like a novel. Its authors were two Chicana professors who fell in love over food: red chile tofu enchiladas, vegetarian pozole. But then one was diagnosed with breast cancer, and food became scary to them. Then I read these lines and heard my ancestors talking to me through the pages: "In Mexican healing traditions, there's a condition called susto, a fright, which startles the spirit from the body. One of the ways of treating this is to cover a person's body with soil to reconnect them to the earth, to this life."[2]

To heal themselves from the susto of breast cancer, the authors put their hands in the earth and started building their own garden and rebuilding their lives. Could cooking help me heal the susto of my ancestors?

I thought immediately of Grandma Cookie. When she was pregnant with my mother, my mom's little fetus womb already held her lifetime supply of eggs, one of which was me. So what my grandmother was feeling at the time of her pregnancy had an effect on me too. Could it be that, newly married, she was terrified to be a mother and to cook and nurture, especially when no one had ever done that for her? She never knew her mother; she was des-madred. Maybe the unsureness I felt in the kitchen was the fear she felt?

I thought about being des-madred while I tried the old-school pinto bean recipe from *Decolonize Your Diet*. It called for only seven ingredients: olive oil, onion, garlic, pinto beans, water, Mexican oregano, and salt. I thought I could handle that. There was an option to cook in a slow cooker, so I pulled out the brand-new one Paloma had bought me last year. As the beans simmered, I thought about my mom, who let her beans cook for hours in a big silver pot while she added beer and cilantro and lots of bacon. I could picture her there now, dancing around our kitchen and listening to her favorite oldies station. I had always thought my mom was a bad cook, but she wasn't. She was mostly just a busy mom, like me, who tended to rush through most things. But even though she was always a whirlwind, she was *there* with us: laughing, dancing, cooking. But after my father died, my mom left too, physically, mentally, and emotionally. Her spirit, her flavor, was gone.

As I gently stirred my simmering beans, it hit me that I had always looked to our dad's death as our big susto. But the truth is that we were dis-mothered too. When my mom emotionally disappeared, the laughter and smells in our kitchen dried up, and we all drifted. Cradling the beans in my ladle as tenderly as if they were my own babies, I thought of Lupe, who cooked and cared for others' children but moved heaven and earth to ensure her girls wouldn't get left behind.

I hungered for that safe feeling we had when my mom's frijoles were cooking on the gas stove, when our parents were happy, and all was good in our cozy little home. I wanted this warm feeling for my own girls, who I felt I may have inadvertently dis-mothered with my overwork. I was trying to find my way back to this place of comfort through this map of a recipe, but I ran out of time. The directions called for the legumes to cook for six hours, but I had to pull them out of their womb-like stew in just four. It was dinnertime, and my family was hungry.

Big mistake.

No one ate my frijolitos. The oregano was too strong for the kids, and Lars doesn't like beans. These didn't change his mind. I wanted to like them, but they were too hard. They weren't ready. Cooking requires time, presence, and patience, qualities neither my mom nor I had much of. As my family dug into the tacos, rice, and guacamole I made, I put the beans back in the pot. Like my frijoles friends, my cooking still needed time to warm up.

The next day at Lupe's, I told her about how I undercooked my beans, and she was shocked that I'd used a slow cooker, preferring my mom's old-school, cook-all-day, stove-top way. She stared up at me and rolled her little eyes.

"*Lo siento*, maestra," I told her. "What are we cooking today?"

"Green pozole!"

Yeehaw! I had been dying to have her teach me how to make pozole since I started learning with her. It was number one on my cooking wish list.

Pozole is a traditional Mexican stew, typically eaten at holidays, but it can be enjoyed year-round. Made with hominy, which is a type of tender white corn kernel that is soaked in lye or limestone water to make it soft and puffy, pozoles are as different as the people who make them, but they usually contain pork or chicken, garlic, hominy, chilis, oregano, and a bay leaf. It can then be garnished with shredded cabbage, cilantro, sliced radish, a squeeze of lime, and seasonings.

Lupe was making a green pozole from tomatillos, serrano, and poblano peppers. We blended a base, then added water, hominy, and pieces of pork. Then I stirred, stirred, stirred to keep the pozole from sticking. It smelled delicious, and when we were done, I asked Lupe for a vegan version. She suggested I make a red version, which had more chilis to give the soup more flavor. I thanked her, gave her a kiss, then headed out the door.

Her recipe called for guajillo peppers, which is a tangy, fruity, medium-spiced pepper. I drove to three different stores but couldn't find them, so I settled on New Mexican peppers, which I thought were a good substitution. I blended the tomato, garlic, and the diced and deseeded pepper. To that base, I added a bay leaf, thyme, Mexican oregano, water, and hominy.

The pozole was tasting really bland, so I threw in another New Mexican pepper. After a while, I dipped my wooden spoon into the pozole and tasted it, but still nothing. So I added more salt, and finally I added a diced pepper. I was free-forming here, but nothing seemed to be popping.

After simmering for a long while, it was as done as it was gonna get. I tested it on Lars and the kids, whom I had yet to win over, and Lars took a spoonful. "It's too peppery for me," he declared in his straightforward Swedish way. Lucia and Astrid just looked scared. This crowd of judges was tough. No more bites were taken. Damn.

Maybe the gods were mocking me by making my meatless vegan pozole so bland. Regardless, I was over it. But between Lupe and my decolonizing cookbook, I could now confidently make home-made pinto beans, Mexican rice, tostadas, stuffed poblano peppers, portabella fajitas, and spicy green beans, all from scratch and all vegan.

To my surprise and joy, I found that my new vegan diet was aligned with a traditional Mexica diet, which was primarily plant based and consisted of corn, beans, squash, wild greens, cactus, fruit, nuts, and seeds. The Mexica didn't have great access to meat, so they ate it very sparingly. And wheat, beef, cheese, cooking oils, and sugar were brought in after colonization. I was interested to learn that the more Latinxs acculturated and ate an American diet, the higher the risk of cancers, heart disease, and diabetes, the last of which is a plague in our community and something both my grandfather and mom had.

I called my mom to check in and brag about my new cooking prowess. Being in the kitchen made me miss her. She was happy and surprisingly interested. I was getting the sense that I was inspiring her to cook, and I wished she lived closer.

I asked her what her favorite dish was, and to my surprise, she said *capirotada*, which is a strange, strange dessert made with white bread, raisins, and longhorn cheese. I wish she wouldn't have said that. She used to make pans of it, and no one would eat it except my grandpa. "I used to make it for my father because he loved it so much," she remembered.

Though it might be the most unappealing recipe I'd known to date, I committed to making capirotada in honor of my mom.

I set off to find the ingredients at a Latino grocery store and spent nearly an hour inside walking the aisles, admiring all the flavors of Takis, produce like nopales, jicama, and plantains, and tons and tons of dried chilis, many of which I'd never heard of.

It was late when I got back, so I made dinner, then put the girls to bed. Lying in their bed, I almost fell asleep but was stricken with the idea that I needed to make the capirotada right away. I dragged myself out of their bed and walked softly downstairs to the kitchen. Though it was only nine o'clock, it was as quiet as if it was the middle of the night. In this silence, I began boiling the piloncillo, cinnamon, and cloves to make the syrup. I then started toasting the *bolillos*, or white rolls. Once all was done, I layered my pan with sliced white bread, drizzled the syrup, and topped it with raisins, pecans, and grated longhorn cheese. My mom and grandpa both loved pecans, so those were an homage to them. I was breaking my new veganism for this recipe, and that was okay. I let that sit for ten minutes, then layered again. After the third layer, I put it in the oven.

Like pozole, there are as many ways to make capirotada as there are makers, and you often used what you had on hand. In that aspect, in *Woman Who Glows in the Dark*, Elena Avila actually compared Curanderismo to capirotada in the sense that when it comes to healing, you use whatever herbs and tools are readily available.

Lars walked in just as I popped the dish in the oven, and he stood with me in the kitchen, waiting for it to be done. We chatted about the girls and school, and I made him laugh by sharing my adventures in Lupe's kitchen. In our late-night cooking session, we were connecting in a way we never could in the chaos of day. It was a warm feeling, and I was almost disappointed when the timer went off. I handed Lars a fork, and we both took a taste of the capirotada right out of the pan. We looked at each other and smiled—it was delicious! The syrup wasn't as thick as the egg custard used in bread pudding, and Lars said he liked the longhorn cheese because the saltiness kept the dessert from being too cloying.

"I owe my mother an apology!" I said to Lars, laughing. "This is *so* good! I had no idea!"

Lars stayed up to help me clean, and we discussed maybe adding more cinnamon or maybe substituting pears for raisins. "You're a good baker," he said sweetly. Mama Natalia and her daughters were bakers. Taking one more spoonful of yummy capirotada, I considered that maybe I was too.

Later that week, I was back in the kitchen, ready to take on pozole again. As I sautéed and heated and stirred the savory pot, I felt possessed, like a witch tending to my brew. It was telling that I had been drawn to soups and broths: chileatole, frijoles, pozoles. I thought of Mama Natalia, who fed the spirit of generations of family with her meals, and of my grandmother Cookie, whose refusal to cook was an act of rebellion. Then I considered my mom, who as a single mom was burdened by cooking. As I stewed and simmered, opening channels and fighting through currents, I knew all these beautiful and powerful women flowed to me, lived in me. They were what gave me my flavor.

I served the pozole for dinner with tostadas. The girls went crazy for the tostadas, which are really just giant tortilla chips. They even gave me their little two thumbs-up signs. Then I poured Lars a piquant bowl of pozole and tried to act cool. We talked about a birthday party Lucia would be attending and Astrid's new day care teacher. Then Lars got up and went to the kitchen and served himself *another* bowl.

"You want more?" I asked incredulously.

"I like it," Lars declared simply. I almost started crying. And in that moment, I got it. For me, these three weeks had been about reclaiming, remembering, and remothering. Passing down and passing on. In Mexica traditions, the hearth was the heart of the home. In making meals for, and from, my family, I filled my heart again, because the kitchen is a place of love. Whether it was home-made pozole or hot dogs, cooking was an offering, like my favorite poem from Hafiz:

And love Says,
"I will, I will take care of you," To everything that is
Near.

Get Rooted Practice #6
Make a Traditional Recipe

"Food is a sense of connection. Food connects me both to Mother Earth but also to my ancestors. I can feel their presence when I'm cooking something that I know my grandmother used to cook."

—Luz Calvo, coauthor of *Decolonize Your Diet*

Whether you grew up with relatives in the kitchen making tamales, cornbread, or gingersnaps, or are more like me and looking to reclaim culture—and a little kitchen confidence—the act of cooking is a joyful way to reconnect with your heritage.

Whether it's your grandmother's dumplings or a wonderful dish you've only heard about, pick a recipe from your ancestry, learn about it, and make it. Cooking uses all our senses and can also serve as a sacred portal that transports us back home through the act of kneading masa or smelling fragrant and familiar spices. Connect with family members to share stories, recipes, and recommendations. Recruit your kids to help you if you can.

Will you learn something about your family, your culture, or yourself that you never knew? Will you keep the recipe as is, or will you substitute ingredients based on availability or preference? Remember that you are allowed to update the recipe. By deciding which ingredients to add, and which to leave out, you are making a recipe all your own.

If making a dish from your culture isn't connecting for you for whatever reason, my friend Lupe shared her delicious chileatole recipe to try.

Lupe's Chileatole Recipe

INGREDIENTS:

6 fresh ears of corn
Water as needed
Sea salt to taste
2–3 green serrano peppers, whole, to taste
3 five-inch stems of epazote or three tablespoons of dried epazote
½ cup instant corn masa mix
1 cup chopped spinach

DIRECTIONS:

1. *Peel and cut one corn into pieces or ¼-inch slices.*
2. *Shell or separate the rest of the corn into kernels.*
3. *Bring 4½ cups of water (2 liters) to a boil, and when ready, add corn and salt. Lower to medium heat and cook corn for 20 minutes, stirring constantly.*
4. *In the blender, grind the peppers, epazote, masa, and spinach with 2 cups of water.*
5. *Add this mixture to the corn, and continue boiling for 10 minutes.*
6. *Salt to taste.*

Remember, you need the consistency to be creamy and thick enough to coat the back of a spoon, not too liquid.

Buen provecho!

6

The Smoking Mirror

Did you know that wolves have twenty-one types of howls? They howl to voice that danger is approaching or to show their location to a member of their pack who might have gotten lost. Wolves even howl to show affection, yelping more often at those they are closest to. While we often think of the lone wolf stoically howling at the moon, most wolves are social souls who howl to protect their pack.

My dad's name, Adolph (Adolfo in Spanish), means "noble wolf," and he was a creature who loved his family fiercely. My dad was also an avid animal lover—we grew up with cats and chickens and rabbits and even a goat, but dogs were by far my father's favorite. When he was a young boy, he always took in strays, annoying the heck out of my stern grandma. But my dad was her *rey*, her king, and despite herself, she allowed his favorite pet, Rinny, to sleep inside their tiny four-room house on cold winter nights. Rinny was my dad's best friend, and when they both got older, my dad would tenderly massage his fur to ease his arthritis.

When Rinny died, my dad was devastated, but he wasn't allowed to cry. His macho father, Geraldo (whose name means "spear"), and the pervasive machismo Mexican culture he was raised in forbade crying. My dad was expected to be a man, and to be a man meant to be rough and tough and fierce—like a weapon. So to mourn his beloved pet and companion, my dad took a large bath towel, draped it over his head, and sat on a chair crying soundlessly.

No sobs or wails escaped; only the shuddering of his skinny shoulders conveyed his grief.

As I sought to know and understand my father, I replayed that Rinny story again and again. And I kept coming back to the same question: What happens to a wolf when it's unable to howl?

"Fuuuck!" I yelped as I tripped on a rock and landed hard on my knee.

I had been running in the woods near my house, trying to shake off a disturbing conversation I'd had with my cousin Patty, when, totally distracted, I ate it—hard. Not only was Patty training to be a curandera, but she also had a master's degree in social work, and I had called her, wanting to talk about my grandfather.

My cousin Flo had confided to me that my grandfather molested her when she was young. In fact, when Patty, Flo, and I had taken a Curanderismo class together, we practiced doing a soul retrieval on Flo.

Our maestro, Bob, asked Flo for all of the names and nicknames she'd had as a child, and then she laid down and the class made a circle around her and lovingly started calling her by the names she recalled, asking her to come back. One name that held particular pain for her was *prieta linda*, or "dark, pretty one," as my grandfather used to call her. "Come back, prieta linda," we whispered. "It's safe. We love you. Come back!" During the retrieval, Flo was crying and moaning and shaking intensely. Afterward, we wrapped her tenderly in a blanket, and Patty and I sat with her as she came into her body.

Flo's admission that our grandfather had molested her as a child was not the first time I had ever heard this about my grandfather. He had died when I was just one year old, and the photo of him that sat on a shelf in my grandma's small house always gave me the creeps. Maybe it was because he wasn't smiling in the picture. Or maybe it was in the whispers of the cousins who said he had done bad things to the family. But diving back into the river of ancestry,

I had begun to think about my grandfather Geraldo and the fact that he was a molester. And more specifically, how did this affect my dad?

When I called Patty to talk it through, she shared that years prior, an older relative had told her that our grandfather had molested other members of the family.

I felt sick as I started spotting clues to a mystery I wasn't sure I wanted to uncover. Patty continued talking about books I should read on molestation and trauma, but I was only half listening, still trying to grasp what she had shared. I was hearing it, but I couldn't fully take it all in yet.

Back on the phone, Patty said something that caught my attention. "When I was little," she said, "I thought Spanish was the language of secrets because the adults would speak in Spanish when they talked about Grandpa and what he had done." Spanish was the language in which they could speak their truth without the children understanding.

As I picked myself up from my fall, I thought, "How can we have a family healing when no one will admit they've been hurt?" I couldn't *force* my relatives into admitting their painful memories. Yet as agonizing as it was to hear about this, and as much as I didn't want to delve further, what rattled me the most about all of this was the continued generational silence.

I might be new to Curanderismo, but I knew intimately how susto worked. You can be silent all you want, but that shit does not go away. So where does susto go when you die? Does it get buried with its victim—or does it get passed down with other traits like brown hair and the ability to draw, inherited like an unwanted gift?

It was the thought of healing my injured bloodline that led me to Albuquerque, New Mexico, on a hot, harried morning. "We have to pick up Sandra and Joey! They're coming too," said Patty. During that revealing conversation, Patty told me about an upcoming Curanderismo training in New Mexico, and I knew that I had to go. So after checking in with Lars and arranging some day camps for the kids, I flew to Albuquerque and was now driving with Patty to our first day of class.

The retreat was held every summer and brought in curanderxs and healers from all over the United States, Mexico, Central and South America, the Caribbean, and Africa. It was an amazing opportunity because Curanderismo is usually passed down within families or via apprenticeships. To be taught this wisdom in a person-to-person setting was a truly rare experience.

I got chills just looking at the syllabus, which offered everything from the history of Curanderismo, to classes focusing on specific conditions like susto or empacho, to lectures on topics like Mayan abdominal massage and healing with the Aztec sun stone. In addition to the bevy of classes, they also offered hands-on workshops on various healing modalities, like fire cupping and how to make herbal tinctures. And they would be holding *temazcal* ceremonies, where people gathered to purge, sweat, and pray.

Soon Patty and I pulled up to a run-down hotel in a not-so-great part of town to pick up the rest of our crew: Patty's high school friend Sandra and Sandra's son, Joey. Patty, Sandra, and Joey had all driven here to Albuquerque from San Antonio, where Sandra and Joey still lived. Best friends since high school, Patty was a *madrina*—godmother—to all Sandra's children. Patty and Sandra brought Joey to the Curanderismo training in the hopes it would inspire him.

Joey was a recovering heroin addict. And when I first saw him as we pulled into the parking lot of their motel, I thought he looked like a young Danny Trejo. He had long braids; a bandanna headband; multiple piercings; and tattoos everywhere, including one on the inside of his lips that read, "Fuck You." I introduced myself as he climbed into the back seat next to me and handed me a waffle he had made in the lobby breakfast area. Munching on the waffle, I noticed a discarded needle on the ground, and all decided it would be best if Sandra and Joey switched hotels.

When we arrived at the university, we saw people gathering on the grass and rushed to join the spiritual opening ceremony. Everyone was gathered in a circle, singing to the beat of the *huehuetl* (drum) and the rattling *sonaja* (rattle), chanting a song: "Heya, heya, heeya, heya heya, heeya. Bienvenidos, bienvenidos, bienvenidos, abuelitos." I joined in the song to greet our abuelos, who would be with us that week as we learned our ancestral medicine, keeping the traditions alive.

The main leader in the circle was a glowing older woman named Rita, who spoke only Spanish. She wore a beautifully embroidered white Mexican dress with a red woven sash and a red band around her head.

After the ceremony calling in the directions, Rita walked around blessing everyone by shaking a bouquet of wet flowers at them like a baptismal. When she came to me, I stood there with my arms outstretched and was sprinkled by the water, which felt refreshing. Even at nine o'clock in the morning, the temperature was eighty degrees and climbing. One more flick of her wrist, and along with the mist, a flower petal came loose and landed in my hair. It felt like a good sign.

Our first lecture of the day was from professor and author Dr. Eliseo Torres—or Cheo, as he was known. Cheo was responsible for putting this course together, and for the past eighteen years, he had brought esteemed academics and healers here from all over the world. Apparently, there was usually a huge contingent from Mexico who drove up for the conference, but they couldn't attend this year because of the visa issues created by the Trump administration.

Cheo lectured on the most famous curanderos, like the legendary El Niño Fidencio. He was called El Niño, or boy, because much like the Dalai Lama, his spirit was joyous like a child's. There is a whole group of devotees who believe in his continued ability to heal, and they call themselves Fidencistas, making an annual pilgrimage to his tomb in the town of Espinazo, located in northern Mexico.

Cheo also spoke about another curandero named Don Pedrito, who was famous for the simple remedies he doled out, like instructing patients to drink more water or immerse an ailing limb in the mud. By the end of the lecture, what I learned more than anything from these celebrated curanderos was that handy medicine from nature could be the most potent healer and that nothing—absolutely nothing—will work without faith. You must believe.

I also perked up when Cheo explained that not everyone needed to be born with the don, or "gift," of healing. It was the *ganas*, or want, as well as the training, that truly made you a skilled curandero. Looking up at the slides of these historic curanderxs, I didn't truly know if I had all the gifts, but I had the ganas, and that was a start.

After lunch, Rita led the first workshop, "Creating Healing and Sacred Spaces." It was beautifully translated by her coteacher, Toñita, who was a local and well-respected curandera. I had created my own sacred space, but learning from Rita, this simple idea of how to create an altar became a three-hour opus on how to heal.

Rita began by explaining that an altar is a place where you go to connect with spirit, with Mother Earth, and to your own roots and culture. Here is where you bow to them all and ask for guidance. She told us that as Latinxs, and society at large, we have lost the connection to our ancestors and culture, and that is why we feel unbalanced. *Equilibrar*—or balance—is a word I would hear again and again over the week. As I listened to loving Rita share these tools, I also thought of being des-madred as we moved away from our medicines.

To demonstrate how to create a sacred, healing space, Rita invited the youngest person in the room to come up to the stage. A young man of seventeen approached, and I was surprised and impressed that he was learning to be a curandero. He even brought his own medicine bag up to the stage. When I was seventeen, I'm pretty sure I was communing with spirits by drinking wine coolers and smoking blunts, but everyone clearly has their own way to transcend.

Rita then asked the oldest female and male to come up. She handed the woman in her seventies an ear of corn and motioned to her to pass it on to the boy. The kernels represented seeds, and it was the elder's job to pass them from one generation to the next. Then she gave the older man a spiky plant, which looked like aloe, that he then handed to the boy. They were symbolically passing on their knowledge, passing on their medicina. Rita reminded us that this medicine was our sacred right. "Now the boy, like a surgeon, has his tools," she explained.

Now, she instructed, we must try the medicine on ourselves. Does rosemary work? Does sound healing with a conch or drum work? "The person we have to work with the most is within," she said. "You don't apprentice with a person; you apprentice with the medicine. When you make a call to learn, the medicine comes like a hummingbird."

At our altar, we feel the strength of our ancestors and their guidance. "When you have doubts or questions, go to the altar!" commanded Rita.

So with "clean hands, ready eyes, and a strong heart," Rita told us, we could begin assembling our own medicine bag, *poco a poco*, inspired by our ancestors, but with our own tools, based on our own earned knowledge and intuition. Over time, our bag grows. And then we, like the boy, will leave it for another generation. And that is the magic. Rita looked out at the audience as I was writing furiously, trying to take it all in, in my eager pocha, academic way. Rita looked straight at me and said in Spanish, "You didn't come to write; you came to feel."

I put my pen down.

Sandra and Joey played hooky the next day, so just Patty and I went to class. We stopped by a store to buy some dried chilis and arrived late to the lecture hall just as two women were setting up their drums. One was a Boricua from the Bronx, who explained that she first started drumming to battle her depression. The other was a Chicana carpenter who wanted to learn more about her Native American ancestry. They shared the physical and emotional benefits of drumming—from reducing inflammation to lowering stress. Research shows that drumming synchronizes the left and right hemispheres of your brain, strengthening your intuition. Most importantly, they explained, drumming was the medicine of the heart.

I found this to be true because as they began playing, I started to cry. The simple drumbeat was so primal, it reverberated right to my core. As tears filled my eyes, my late uncle Oscar, who was shot and killed as a teenager, came into my mind.

My tía Ximena told me a story about how after they found out Oscar had died, my grandmother sent her and my dad to pick up shoes my grandmother was having repaired. When my grandmother had dropped them off, she could never have imagined that she'd need them to wear to the funeral of her firstborn son. As my dad and aunt were walking home down the busy downtown street, they both burst into tears. They couldn't help it. People stopped to ask them what was wrong, but, too overwhelmed with grief, they couldn't answer and just kept on walking and crying, carrying the polished shoes my grandmother would wear to Oscar's funeral.

I was still thinking of my dad and his siblings when Patty and I sat down for an obsidian mirror workshop.

From our teacher, we learned obsidian is a volcanic glass used by Mexica for weapons—and for ritual. In class, we worked with an obsidian mirror, which was a disk about five inches in diameter (they can be bigger or smaller) used for divination and healing. Later, I read that Queen Elizabeth I famously had a court "conjurer" who used an obsidian mirror from Mexico to conjure spirits and tell the future. Our maestro told us that obsidian represents the strength of Tezcatlipoca. Tezcatlipoca is the ruler of the north and is called the Smoking Mirror. Tezcatlipoca represents our shadow sides and our connections to our guiding ancestors. When you look into his smoky obsidian mirror, he casts a light on that which usually stays hidden. Wow.

Up until now, I had been enjoying my time in the direction of the north: calling in my ancestors, learning about our untold history, and reclaiming the old ways. But I was learning the north is also the place of darkness, a place of things hidden or purposely left unseen.

I understood now that in dealing with ancestry, there is no way we can resurrect familial gems without also surfacing our family muck—the negative habits, patterns, and ways that pierce through generation after generation like poisoned arrows. It made sense I had stumbled onto this family secret of my grandfather being a molester. In the direction of the north, people and secrets long hidden were coming to light.

In our workshop, our instructor said we used the mirror to take control of our consciousness. Obsidian, he said, helps us connect with our innermost self, our dark side, so that we can see our whole truth. We practiced working with the mirror, and I was trying to focus on these techniques as I held the cool sphere in front of me. But when I looked in the mirror, I just kept seeing the unsmiling face of my grandfather, which made me want to shut my eyes.

I woke up the next day exhausted after a fitful night of sleep and was quiet and moody when we picked up Sandra and Joey for class. Joey had missed all of yesterday's activities, and Patty was disappointed. We all needed this healing work, especially him. Trying to get out of my own head, I asked Joey how he slept.

"Not well," he replied as we pulled into the parking lot.

"How come?" I asked. As we got out of the car and walked toward class together, he told me he had nightmares. Sandra and Patty walked on, but sensing Joey wanted to share, I stopped outside the classroom to talk to him.

He told me he had a dream his "baby mama" and son were zombies. They were dead, and he couldn't wake them up or save them. Upset, he began to tell me about his son and his ex-girlfriend, whom he had dated since he was fifteen—half his life.

When she became pregnant, they tried to be a family, but soon they broke up. Joey, who was trying desperately to quit using, hadn't seen his son in a while.

He pulled out photos of his little boy and his ex, and as we looked at his *hijo*'s big smile and angelic black curls, Joey said simply, "I don't want to be like this." Beyond his tough-looking demeanor, I could see his tenderness. He told me of the drug-fueled parties he used to have with speedballs of cocaine and heroin.

Listening, horrified, I looked at him and said, "You're so beautiful. Why would you do that to yourself, mijo?"

He looked at me and shook his head. We were both crying as I put my arms around him. Something in Joey made me think of my father. His humor, his sensitivity, alongside his tormenting sustos. And the weight of carrying it all, expected to be a tough Latino. A spear.

I knew I had to take Joey to see Virginia. My new maestra lived in Albuquerque, but besides a quick hug and hello, we hadn't had the time for a good heart-to-heart platica. And honestly, I needed a limpia desperately. I knew Joey needed one too. So that's how we found ourselves knocking on the door of a church.

Virginia greeted us quietly and led us upstairs to her healing room. Joey and I sat across from her on a couch, kinda awkwardly—like partners in couples counseling—as she explained to Joey who she was and what she did. She asked us if we had any questions, which we didn't, and after some silence, we decided that I would get a limpia first.

Virginia and I spent a good forty-five minutes doing our platica and catching up. I told her what I had learned about my grandfather as she listened quietly. "You mentioned that my dad died of anger. Now I know why," I told her. I recounted my tía Ximena's memory of her and my dad walking down the street, crying over the death of his brother. I thought about the molestation in our family. The fact that my father's father was a sexual predator and no one talked about it. Loved ones of people who have been abused talk about a double kind of trauma: the trauma of witnessing something horrific, but also the trauma of feeling helpless to stop it.[1] I felt this agonizing impotence with my own sisters.

"You should get a small drum," Virginia suggested, "and vocally release your anger and sadness, the way your dad never could." I told her how moved I had been by the drumming in class. How, when they played them, I cried.

"Get your drum, comadre, and beat into the feelings of anger, of helplessness, of worthlessness, and break them apart so you can move into being a woman of power!"

I was surprised when she used the word *power* because, at that moment, I felt so very small.

When it was time for my limpia, she motioned me to a massage table, where I laid faceup and closed my eyes. Then she started playing her drum and singing softly. I don't know how long it lasted, but the drumming put me in a trance. Soon, I started to have a vision: I was at the hospital where my dad died. I was back in the memory of my gran susto where my dad was sick, and instead of taking care of him, I left his bedside to climb onto a roof and read by myself.

But now, in my vision, my dad wasn't lying weak in his hospital bed. He was healthy and walking toward me. His face was shining with love. He walked to the waiting room and opened the window to the roof where I was sitting. He looked at me and said, "It's time to come in, mija." He held my hand and helped me down from where I had been hiding. And as I stood in front of him, we embraced hard, and he said, "I'm here, I'm always here."

"We did good work today," Virginia said when I came back to the room and told her what I had seen.

I nodded in agreement, crying, and hugged her, placing my head on her left shoulder. Heart to heart.

I went outside, seeking air, as Joey entered her room. I saw a beautiful little labyrinth set up in the yard and walked through the spiraling stone path, finding a white feather on the way. I picked it up and kept walking. At the end was an altar, and I gave my feather as an offering. "Thank you, thank you, thank you," I whispered as I knelt to the ground.

About forty-five minutes later, I was sitting on a bench when Joey and Virginia came out the door, both of them looking startled. "We brought a lot of stuff up," she said to me as I looked at Joey, who was in tears. He sat down, and I put my arm around him. "He needs a deep soul retrieval with Laurencio. He needs to be buried."

Laurencio was a masterful curandero from Oaxaca who gave a class on soul retrievals. To shed very deep, deep trauma, like sexual abuse, curanderos can bury a person in the ground up to their neck.

They stay with them, wiping away any bugs and making them feel safe. The idea is that Mother Earth can take the trauma, even an ugly, heavy one.

This was what she was recommending for Joey. She also suggested he visit an acupuncturist to get detox needles in his ear. I listened and thanked her and looked at Joey, who was still crying. "I told her everything," he said, "about my son, and my family, and the drugs."

"I'm proud of you, papa," I told him.

He looked at me and nodded, then headed over to the labyrinth, where he began trying to find his way.

At the end of the week, we all went to a temazcal at the curandera Toñita's house, a welcoming adobe-style *casita*. People were milling in her backyard, and I went to check out the temazcal, a small, round clay hut that looked like a burning-hot igloo. Next to the temazcal was a shrine to La Virgen de Guadalupe, and I remembered what someone told me earlier about temazcals being "feminine."

It made sense that temazcals would be feminine, as they are supposed to resemble the womb—round and dark. It even had a tiny hole at the top, kind of like a whale's blowhole, that was supposed to symbolically represent the belly button. After a ceremony and limpia, we all filed into the temazcal one by one, sitting on the built-in clay bench that ran the perimeter of the temazcal. It fit twenty-one people max but was crowded by the time the tenth person crawled in. "How in the heck will we all fit in?" I wondered. Skin to sweaty skin was how.

Rita let us know we could leave at any time, but instead I moved to sit on the floor, which was cooler. Once we were situated, Rita entered and started playing the drum while leading us through a meditation. A temazcal is a tool for purification, a place to let go of unwanted feelings or emotions. Rita instructed us to take a deep breath, then scream out anything we didn't need. At first, I made some sort of feeble moan, but soon I heard Joey scream, then Sandra, and Patty too. It was weird; I felt as if I was inside the eye of the storm, sitting quietly while others yelled around me.

How many times had I done this? Stayed quiet when people around me were hurting and howling? How many times had I stayed silent when I was hurting and howling inside, instead smiling and saying, "It's okay"? This was a learned generational habit, a legacy of lying to ourselves. I thought of my susto habit of overworking and overdrinking to the point of bleeding on my clothes and trying to pretend it was all okay. Of my mother never uttering a word about Lety's substance use. I thought of little Apolonia and Paloma crying for their papa to come home. And I thought of my dad and how he couldn't cry about his dog dying or the abuse in his family. And all the horrors that came before: genocides, rapes, and the incalculable loss of culture. I felt the darkness in the pit of my belly, and then I felt the rise and the open. I started howling at the top of my lungs. I howled about my dad, my grandfather, my sisters, my cousins, abused people everywhere, Joey's struggles, the oppressive heat, the dark river of susto that just kept flowing from one generation to the next. I howled what felt like centuries of unheard screams, and next to me, my pack howled right back.

I woke up the next day with my jaw sore from screaming, but I felt undeniably light as Patty and I started getting ready for class. Today was my last day; I would be flying home that night. "I have some-thing for you," Patty said, handing me a small paper bag. I pulled out two red sashes, the kind curanderas wear for ceremony and protection. I ran my fingers over the ribbed, woven fabric.

"Thank you," I said, giving her a hug. I put on a white sundress and tied one of the sashes around my waist. I was ready to take my place.

Get Rooted Practice #7

Healing Baño

Healing with water is a sacred and ancient rite, and while we don't all have access to a temazcal, we can still create our own cleansing ritual with *baños*,[2] which are sacred herbal baths. They are a type of limpia, and you can create a healing baño whether you want to shed the stresses of your day or need an infusion of love and protection.

I like to light candles around my bathtub (daytime or night) as the flame symbolizes transformations and helps us connect to our divine guides.

Traditional cleansing herbs are rosemary, basil, sage, and rue. Flowers (like roses) are beautiful for heart healing and sadness. Mexican marigolds bring supportive grandmother energy. Yarrow offers protection.

I adore rosemary; it speaks to me. It is protective yet loving and is said to strengthen self-love as well as fortify your heart and willpower.

The choosing of the plants for your baño is part of your healing. I suggest that you don't overthink it, but rather choose what calls to you.

Fill your tub with hot water, not unbearable but nice and hot.

You have two choices for steeping herbs. You can boil the herbs in a large pot on the stove, then let them simmer for an hour; when they cool, pour them over yourself as you stand in your shower or bathtub. Or you can add the herbs directly to your bath. Both are lovely. I usually do the latter because I like the relaxation of soaking in a bath, but you will need a good mesh drainer, and be prepared to clean the tub after!

You can add bath salts or Epsom salts (magnesium sulfate) and essential oils to your baths for extra relaxation.

Once you ease yourself into the bath, unwind and breathe as the warmth and herbs envelop your body. If you're inspired, you can say your intentions or what you need to let go of out loud. You might be called to sing or feel the need to release with a cry—or maybe you just need to relax and luxuriate in the warm water like a baby in the womb.

When you feel done, wrap yourself in a cozy robe and drink a nice hot cup of herbal tea. The warmth helps you to continue cleansing and releasing, and self-tenderness is part of the ritual to come back to again and again.

PART THREE

The West: How to Let That Shit Go, for Real This Time

7

Building Your Medicine Bag

"Babe, where is all my sage?" I asked Lars as I stared at an empty patch of soil.

"Oh, I pulled it out so I could plant some more lettuce," he said, making little holes with his fingers in the now-bare earth, where he was carefully dropping seeds for greens.

"Why?" was all I could muster as I took in what used to be rows upon rows of velvety green herbs.

"We had so much, and we never used it." Lars sounded defensive, as if sensing trouble.

"I used it! I was growing sage to use for cleansings in my practice! It's one of my tools!"

"I'm sorry!" said Lars. "I didn't know!"

"Why didn't you take the thyme? Look at all that stupid thyme!" I pointed to the now annoyingly huge patch of thyme sprigs. "I've only used it for onion soup!" This was a dig at Lars, who loves onion soup.

"There's still some sage left," he replied hopefully, pointing at a few remaining stalks.

As I headed back inside the house, a voice whispered, "You didn't tell him it was important." Whether it was Mama Natalia or just my own brain, I didn't know, but it was true. Months into my reclamation journey, and I was still hiding.

Three weeks earlier, I had come back from New Mexico feeling as churned up as the dirt I now hoed in my garden to plant new sage. During the powerful retrieval with Virginia, I had felt a piece of my soul click back into place. Yet the discovery of my grandfather's abuse—and the questions it raised—made me feel as yanked and uprooted as the pesky weeds I was clearing. And unexpectedly, now that I had retrieved a part of myself, I could acutely see—and feel—other sustos. Memories of jobs and relationships I stayed in too long, hoping I could change what was unchangeable, kept waking me up in the middle of the night, leaving me exhausted and irritable.

And my enhanced "susto spotter" was working overtime on my family. Now that I was trying to heal my own wounds, the hidden—and not-so-hidden—hurts of those around me were glaring. Paloma's stress and anxiety veiled as sarcasm, Lety's tenuous recovery, and Apolonia's constant struggles as a single mom all felt like the volume rising on a ticking bomb I couldn't find.

I was 108 days into my project, almost halfway there, yet I felt I should be further along. I was beyond grateful for all that I had learned in New Mexico. But now back at home, in the mundane madness of my everyday life, I wasn't sure how to make use of any of it. I felt like someone had given me a pouch of magical seeds without instructions for growing them.

"Build your medicine bag; play with the medicina!" Rita had instructed us. But I didn't feel like playing as I ferociously attacked an unyielding clump of dirt. Not when things in my family were still so messed up and the clock was ticking. I needed skills, answers, something to slay this choking susto once and for all.

In my urgency to begin building my medicine bag, I knew I had to dive deeper into learning about medicinal plants. Herbalism is foundational to Curanderismo, and I needed some of that grounding. Luckily, Lars was a natural gardener, and I was an eager apprentice. That summer, we had already grown a bountiful harvest of kale and purple and orange carrots the girls loved pulling right from the ground. Cherry tomatoes twinkled at us, hanging from vines as cheery as Christmas lights, and the cucumbers were so robust, they made me blush.

My mom hadn't been much of a gardener—probably too busy to care for one more living thing. But Mama Natalia had loved her *plantitas.* One of the few memories I have of her is her sweeping her small porch and tending to her potted plants. Dora had told me that Mama Natalia was a big fan of yerba buena (mint) and had considered it a cure-all. Running my hands over the giant stalks of wild mint that grew in my yard, I thought of my 'buelita as I brought my fingers to my nose, inhaling the invigorating fresh scent.

In the Aztec empire, many families had their own gardens for healing and eating called *xochichinancalli,* which means "flower place enclosed by reeds." Inspired by my ancient ancestors, I was establishing my own curandera's corner, where I planted rosemary, basil, and sage. And I spent hours weeding and watering and cheering on my blossoming plants.

Even though gardening was physically exhausting and I had no idea what I was doing most of the time (am I overwatering or underwatering?), I did feel plugged back into life among the plants and dirt and fascinating tiny creatures. And I wanted to learn more.

Studying herbalism, with all of its classifications and contraindications, felt daunting, but I was inspired to do it because now I was moving out of the direction of the north, the place of ancestors— with all of its holy gifts and horrible discoveries—and entering the direction of the west, the place of sunset, earth, vegetation, and renewal.

I signed up for a course taught by a Latinx herbalist who was young enough to be my kid yet as wise and strong as the oak trees that shaded my garden.

A powerful theme of the class was "decolonizing herbalism," which I started to interpret as trusting yourself and establishing a relationship to plants to see what medicine they offered—or didn't. It also meant honoring the knowledge and lived experience of so many healers and grandmothers and mothers and neighbors who might not know the academic Latin names of plants but were still potent wisdom holders.

In our class, we were encouraged to talk to our plants and leave them offerings, like songs or cornmeal. This was a contrast to the colonizer's practice of just taking, trampling, and extracting without any respect or reverence.

I felt embarrassed talking to the plants at first, but soon I found myself praising the *romero* that was growing so strong and kneeling on the ground quizzically, peering into the dirt, asking the corn why she wasn't taking root. Maybe I was turning into that plant-whispering tía I always wished I had. And if so, could I use these tender words and care to help grow myself?

Sitting under our dogwood tree, reading *Infusions of Healing: A Treasury of Mexican-American Herbal Remedies*, I learned the Mexica were master botanists. In 1467, their leader, Motecuhzoma I, created what some believe was the very first botanical garden in the world with nearly two thousand plant species, replete with specially trained gardeners to tend to them. The gardens were created for both aesthetic and medicinal purposes. When the Spanish arrived at the Aztec empire, they were stunned by the floral beauty and the vast knowledge of plant medicine. A Spanish soldier wrote of the majestic gardens he encountered, "I could not get enough of it, the variety of trees and the aroma each one had, of the terraces full of roses and flowers, and the many fruits of the land . . . and I say again, as I stood there admiring it all, I do not believe that in the world there was such a land as this one. Now all of this is fallen, and none of it remains."

What was not ruined and razed by the conquistadors in battle was exterminated by the Catholic church. Libraries of codices and papers filled with medicinal knowledge were destroyed as heresy and paganism. If not for this, the author suggests that Mexico might have rivaled China as a world leader in herbal medicine.[1]

Walking through my yard, I was learning to identify plants that were growing naturally, like mugwort, which can be used to remember your dreams and to ease the itch of bug bites; plantain, which was good for cuts; yarrow, which works to stop bleeding and set boundaries; and wild mint, which is great for digestion and mojitos. I imagined Motecuhzoma's lush, expansive gardens. The care put in, the knowledge cultivated, the beauty and poetry the gardens inspired. And how, in the end, it was all destroyed.

"You need to get your head out of the books, mija, and start practicing in the real world!" Virginia chastised me during a catch-up call when I told her how I had signed up for yet *another* class. Virginia was always trying to get me to apply what I was learning, and I knew she was right. Patty had given me the red sash of the curandera, and despite my nervousness, it was time to start growing into it. Trying to kick-start my Curanderismo practice, I emailed close friends and family, asking for clients to practice on for free, and my wonderful friend Meghann answered immediately.

I pulled rosemary and sage and flowers for her limpia, and when she arrived, I took her upstairs to my altar, where we sat cross-legged for our platica. I asked Meghann what was bothering her and stayed quiet as she talked about her desire to have a baby, her fear of financial instability, and her confusion over her fiancé's reluctance to move forward on nearly anything.

When she stopped talking, I didn't fill the space with my commentary; instead, I gave her the pause and space to go deeper. And she did. Soon we realized what she was really worried about was the uncertainty. Not knowing where the money would come from. Should she take the safe-and-steady $120,000-a-year job, though it was the exact opposite thing her Ser wanted her to do? And when would the baby come? And would the fiancé ever show up in the way she needed him to?

I started the session thinking this was a relationship problem, but soon I understood it was an issue of trust. Meghann needed to root back into herself instead of flying away in susto and worry. In her face, I could see her mind working and whirling. I could feel her incessant questioning and fear. My heart ached in recognition because Meghann wasn't dropping into her own heart and knowing. Looking at Meghann, I could see the knowing stillness beneath the noise, the quiet river of her Ser. She knew what she wanted to do; she just had to trust herself to do it. I wanted to hug Meghann and tell her it would all be all right. And that's when I knew it was time to start the limpia.

As she stood, I held the fresh herbs at the crown of her head and called in Mama Natalia and Meghann's guides to come work through me. Then I swept the stalks down her arms and across her heart, stopping to pray over her womb. Here, I asked La Virgen de Guadalupe—who was sitting on my altar—to banish Meg's fear and plant the seed of strength she would need for the baby and the creative projects that were on the way. I prayed silently to let Meghann feel her power as a mother, so she could begin guiding herself and the baby that would come. At the end, I had her step on the plants. We hugged, left side to left side, heart to heart. Virginia always reminded me that "corazón *cura* corazón." It was true; heart cures heart, and helping Meghann's also helped mine. Meghann would be a mother. She just had to trust herself and her Ser. And maybe one day, I would come into my own as a curandera. Like seeds taking root, we just needed time.

Inspired by my session with Meghann, I called my baby sister to catch her up on everything that had happened these last few weeks. Paloma had a fabulous job as a trend spotter for big fashion brands and was constantly traveling the world. She is the least woo-woo of my sisters, but she is usually supportive of my endeavors, however "out there."

"What a fucking sicko!" Paloma blurted out when, after sharing about my plant studies and trip to New Mexico, I told her about our grandfather. "So you talked to Lety about this?" she asked me.

"Yeah, we spoke last week."

"She thinks you're stirring up trouble," she said.

"What?" I answered, confused.

"Yeah, she called me last week, I guess after she spoke with you, and she was going off, saying that you were digging up all this family drama 'cause you're bored and you needed to get a life."

"What are you talking about?" I said, bewildered and offended at every part of that sentence.

"Relax. She was being kind of funny about it," said Paloma, though I really didn't see anything funny at all.

"It was actually nice to talk to her now that she's sober. We were kind of bonding over making fun of you," Paloma said, trying to explain but not making me feel any better. "Yeah, Lety was complaining about how you don't have any real trauma. 'She hasn't been in prison! She hasn't lost her husband!'" Paloma said, mimicking Lety while mocking me.

"Look, relax, we're just giving you shit. I know you're having a midlife crisis or something." She said it in a way that showed she didn't know what I had been going through at all.

After we hung up, I sank rapidly into a quicksand of doubt. I knew my sisters were just messing with me like they always did. But I always took it because I knew they really loved me, and that roughness was how we talked to each other. I'd always thought they were keeping me "real," but now I wondered if they were just trying to keep me put. My sisters could be my biggest champions, my greatest defenders, always ready to take off the hoops and throw *chingasos* for me. But they could also be my worst critics, landing stinging barbs right into my core.

I realized that here I was, incensed after reading about colonizers stealing and stamping out my culture, but the oppression was also coming from inside the house, deflating my dreams and dismissing my experiences with the steely weapons of sarcasm and shaming.

I started cleaning my office, which was turning into a botanica lined with Ball jars of herbs and salves and liniments. "Am I digging up stuff better left alone?" I asked myself as I shook a jar of fresh oregano steeped in olive oil to keep it from settling. I had long accused my mom of melodrama, but maybe I was the one being dramatic, overfocusing on our susto. It's true; everyone in my family suffered, many much worse than me, and they didn't seem particularly worried about it. Why was I?

I looked around at all of my plant experiments, and instead of feeling pride, they seemed silly. Child's play. Hearing the kids call me from downstairs, I took off the red sash I was wearing and let it fall to the floor.

I had another limpia scheduled for the next day, and unsurprisingly, it didn't go well. My friend showed up late and was very anxious and hyper. Instead of me calming *her* down, she riled *me* up. She kept rattling on, hopping from the boss she hated to her ex she still seemed hung up on, and I never felt like I could get a handle on the platica or how to root her. I tried to ground us both when doing her limpia, but when we were done, she was still as antsy as ever and asked disappointedly, "Was that it?"

The performing part of me almost wanted to pull a rabbit out of a hat to impress her. Instead, I smiled thinly and said, "Yup, that's all I got," directing her out of my house with my sage bundle still in hand like an aircraft marshaller.

"Well, that was a disaster!" I said aloud as I heard her car pull away.

A few days later, I was in desperate need of my own limpia, so I went to visit Laurencio, a curandero I had met in New Mexico and who was visiting clients in New York. Laurencio was a skillful curandero whose specialty was susto, and I was excited to spend time with him where he was staying in Long Island.

Sitting in metal lawn chairs, with the sun sparkling off the water, we began our platica. He asked me about my children and husband. Things had been strained. Healing sustos shakes shit up, and feelings I used to suppress—or bypass—like anger, confusion, and fear, were free flowing now. I wasn't always the happy-happy, joy-joy person I had long pretended to be.

Unfortunately, I couldn't articulate that in my eighth-grade Spanish, so instead, I managed, "I love my family, but sometimes they drive me nuts!" He laughed in agreement.

Laurencio shared that he had two daughters too, who were now grown and helped him with his practice back in Oaxaca. The message I was learning was that this ancestral medicine wasn't just for me, but for my children too. I made a note to ground myself in that truth when I felt shrunken by fear or insecurity in the garden or with my new clients.

I attempted to tell Laurencio about my sisters' struggles, our strained relations, and my own long-standing susto response to escape into busyness or booze. And the damage that remained. "How many soul retrievals do you need before you are finally cured?" I asked Laurencio desperately.

He smiled a kind, knowing smile that was ever so sad. He explained that we can—and will—suffer many sustos, again and again. "From trauma, violations, robberies," he said in Spanish. "But we will learn how to heal them faster, coming back more quickly into ourselves."

I knew then I had to continue with a soul retrieval for my family. We all had so much to heal from.

I must have looked miserable because Laurencio took my hands, looked in my eyes, and told me, "*¡No te preocupes! ¡Disfruta tu vida! Disfruta tus hijas, ellas son tus flores. Tu trabajo es para ayudarles a crecer. Verlos florecer. ¡La vida es bella! ¡Tienes amor! Disfruta. Este es tu don.*"*

He was admonishing me with the wisdom of someone decades older to stop worrying and enjoy my life. I got it, but wasn't that easier said than done when there was still so much suffering close to me?

"Pray and practice the medicina," he told me firmly. Then he stood. It was time for my limpia. He pulled stalks of herbs from a white flower bucket, allowing me to inhale the sweet scent of fresh

---

* "Don't worry! Enjoy your life! Relish your daughters, they're your flowers. Your job is to help them grow. See them blossom. Life is beautiful! You have love! Enjoy it. That is your gift."

basil as he recited a prayer in Spanish asking for God and the angels to cleanse me, to take away any sadness, and to leave me balanced. He started with the top of my head and worked his way down, sweeping the stalks across my body. With every stroke of the yerbas, I exhaled and felt tension and emotions release in the circling wind. He continued the brushing downward until the cleansing stalks were at my feet, and I stepped on them. He then finished by blowing mescal in my face, in the pits of my elbows, and in the nape of my neck. The mescal, I found out later, was to reawaken my central nervous system. Though I smelled like a spring breaker in Cancun, I felt so much lighter and present than when I first arrived.

I hugged Laurencio tightly, hoping his internal sense of peace would infuse all my still-broken places.

The next day I was spraying the kids with the hose in our yard when it occurred to me that I needed my own garden bed. Lars and I had prepped and planted the four beds we had, but after the sage fiasco, we clearly needed to grow.

I explained this to Lars, and throughout the week, he helped me build and prep two more small rectangular beds that would be all mine.

Excited, I bought lavender and rue plants, as well as chamomile and epazote seeds, the latter in honor of my comadre Lupe, who used so much of the pungent herb in her cooking.

Each packet of seeds came with its own care instructions, and while I tended to think about soil, water, and sunlight as the most important factors to a plant's health, it was also important that each plant and seed had enough *space* to grow.

I felt like the space Laurencio had created in my body and mind with his limpia let me see how much space I need everywhere in my life: in my garden, with my sisters, and especially with Curanderismo. In the garden, Lars took up more space. He was better at it, so he had more confidence. He was also a dude, and dudes tend to take up more space, even enlightened Swedish ones.

The same was true with Curanderismo. The image of Mama Natalia loomed large, both on my altar and in my psyche. I needed to step out of her mighty shadow and give myself the space to build my own medicine bag and practice without constantly comparing myself to her.

Laurencio had used the word *don* during our platica. In Spanish, the word *don* refers to our "gifts" or "natural abilities."

Later in my office, I sat in front of my altar and began to dig up my *dones*, making a list of things I was naturally good at, things I loved to do, and things I felt called to do, even if I didn't have any experience in them at all. My list looked like this:

Robyn's Dones
—Mama
—Storyteller
—Sister/comadre
—Plant mama
—Animal ally
—Cloud watcher
—Sun soaker
—Tree hugger
—Fire gazer
—Student
—Book lover
—Yogi
—Breath rider
—Dreamer

Some, obviously, were just for fun, but by writing them down on paper, I saw that I had been calling on and applying my dones throughout my life and career, from stargazing as a kid to telling stories about my community as a journalist and editor.

Once I had written them out in my journal, I began to appreciate my gifts as precious tools to include in my medicine bag. I had thought I was starting out with an empty bag, but as I looked over my list, I understood I had more talents and dones than I gave myself credit for. My practice would look different from Mama Natalia's but not any less worthy.

"What are you doing?" Lety asked sweetly.

Feeling more empowered and spacious, I had called Lety the next morning. I was still hurt from the conversation Paloma had shared, and I didn't want to accumulate any more sustos if I could help it.

"Hey, so Paloma told me y'all were chatting, and you were kind of ragging on the healing work I'm doing right now, and I just want to say that's not cool . . . and it hurt my feelings." I don't think I had ever said those words to any of my sisters. We didn't usually talk to each other like that. Our sustos had made us tough, but I didn't want them to make us hard.

"Well, I was talking to Aunt Paola, and she said you were asking all these questions about Dad and Grandpa, and I was just wondering what you are doing."

"What I am doing is trying to get to know our father better. You were nineteen when he died, but I was only thirteen, and Apolonia was only ten. And Paloma was only seven! And what I found out about Grandpa has everything to do with Dad. It makes a lot of sense now as to why Dad was always so strict, overprotective, and quick to anger. I'm allowed to ask these questions. He was my father."

"I'm not saying you're not allowed," she said defensively. "I just didn't understand."

"And also," I continued, "don't compare our trauma. You have been through a lot. I know you have," I said, softening. "But while you were gone all those years, I was going through a lot too. We *all* were."

Lety was silent for a moment. I didn't fill the gap.

"I'm sorry," she said simply, which I did not expect.

"Look, I've been going through it," I said. "I've been struggling with my drinking, and I'm trying not to drink right now, actually.

And I don't know, my job sucked, and I'm just feeling really lost lately."

She was quiet again for what seemed like the longest we've ever been quiet, and then said, "I went through so much y'all don't even know about." I stayed quiet as she continued. "I just don't want to think that you were suffering too. It hurts me."

"Me too," I said. "It hurts me too."

After we hung up, I thought about how growing up, my sisters and I all needed so much more space than we had: at the table, in the car, in the bathroom, in the ways we were allowed to be outside of the narrow roles our parents assigned to us as "pretty," "smart," "sporty," and "funny."

When my father died and our parents' love and attention was cut in half and divided by four, it felt to me like my sisters' wants and needs and problems took up *so* much space, I didn't have room to act up or shout out or unfurl myself in all the ways I needed. It wasn't their fault. We all just needed more of what every living thing on earth requires: water, light, space, tenderness, and love.

And in this new and reclaimed space to grow and think and be, it occurred to me that maybe *that* was exactly what I was doing for myself with this healing project that no one understood. At times, not even me.

Get Rooted Practice #8

What Is Your Don?

When I started on the path of being a curandera, I read that most curanderas had the don of healing. My great-grandmother Mama Natalia definitely had the don. She was an intuitive, she worked with herbs and the body, and she read cards.

What was less certain—for me, anyway—was whether *I* had the don for healing. I have a keen intuition. I'm deeply spiritual. I love helping people. But does that make me a "natural" healer?

After lots of confusion and research and conversations with other healers, I learned that your don can be something you're born with *and* something you cultivate. My friend Vanessa Codorniu explains it as being "a vessel of karma" or a "vessel of calling."

When she was five, Vanessa started having visions. By sixteen, she was giving psychic readings, and her astrology chart has intuitive healer written all over it. Vanessa believes that she and others like her made a "soul agreement" before birth to come back and heal the world.

Still others grow their intuitive skills from basic to mastery because they've had a calling. This could be spurred on by a dream or dramatic experience or something that set them on the path. I have a friend who survived breast cancer when she was in her thirties. Grateful for the miracle of life, she now works as a sound healer in hospitals because she believes music helped her heal.

I believe that being a curandera is both my don and a calling. So while I have natural abilities in some areas, I work to cultivate other skills.

To help figure out your gifts, write out a list of your dones. Ones that come naturally to you and ones you are called to. Don't edit yourself, and know that this list can and will grow and change over time.

Loving to travel can be a don. Being a mom can be a don. Having a great sense of style can be a don. And what are the things that are calling you? Bread making? Moving to Italy? Taking a singing class?

Your homework is to choose one don and start practicing and playing with it. In Nahuatl, the number one means "the power from which everything emanates."[2] Taking one action has power.

Remember, we begin to build our medicine bags by remembering our own gifts, our own sacred medicine. And honoring our gifts honors the world because gifts are meant to be shared.

Get Rooted Practice #9
Connect with Sunflower Energy

I've always connected with sunflowers, which are native to present-day New Mexico and Arizona. I enjoy sunflower bouquets, and every summer my kids and I grow sunflowers. We give our sprouts fun names like Bud, Buddy, Sprout, Willie, and Millie so we can encourage them as they grow.

I was happily surprised when I learned from my friend and curanderx Atava Garcia Swiecicki that sunflower energy helps to boost self-esteem for those needing to firm up their confidence. They remind us that like radiant sunflowers, we too can stand tall and proud, shine brightly, and take up space.

You can call in the joyous and spacious sunflower energy by

- planting sunflowers,
- making a sunflower flower essence, or
- placing sunflowers on your altar and in your home.

In the morning or when you pass by them, take in their sturdy energy and feel yourself stand stronger as you raise your face to the sun and shine like we are all meant to.

8

Reclaiming Your Worth

"We're going to Mexico!"

I had just hung up the phone with Rita the curandera, who had a small healing center on the outskirts of Mexico City. Although I was annoyed with two of my sisters and disconnected from the third, I still hoped to carry on with our family soul retrieval.

I looked out the window, admiring the leaves that were starting to turn fiery red and golden. As I breathed in the invigorating fall breeze, I could feel the change in the air, and I was ready for it.

"Does everyone have passports?" was the first question Lars asked when I told him about my big travel plans over dinner of *calabacitas*. Calabacitas (little squash) is a traditional Mexican dish of sautéed squash, onions, garlic, and corn that my mom used to make.

I didn't answer Lars's question, instead turning to slice fresh jalapeños picked from the garden, feeling myself getting as heated. I was so excited that Rita, a seasoned curandera, had the time, space, and willingness to accommodate us. I hadn't even thought about passports! Why was Lars trying to bring me down with trifling practicalities?

Instead of answering, I retorted with a question of my own: "Have you cut the grass yet?" I asked sweetly as I stabbed a piece of squash with my fork.

Astrid's birthday was two weeks away. The weather in fall is glorious in the Northeast, and we were having a big outdoor party for her, with pumpkins and a piñata and lots of games and guests.

We had a good-size yard, yet our lawnmower was a manual-push one from, like, 1930. At first, I thought Lars's hipster weirdness was kind of cute, but since I'd been more on grass-cutting duty, I'd discovered it was actually really annoying. I was officially on strike until we got a new mower. Lars, though, loved his Luddite lawnmower, so we were currently at a stalemate. In the meantime, our grass had grown super long. Just last week, we'd had friends over for a barbecue, and the yard was itchy and full of mosquitoes. It wasn't cute.

"Maybe you can tell me how you plan to pay for your trip?" he retorted as he left the room. Even though I was annoyed as hell, Lars wasn't wrong. I had no idea how I was going to pay for all of us to go to Mexico. It was time for the next item on my list.

A few days later, Vanessa, a curandera and clinical hypnotist, stared hard at me, her eyes framed by her mass of curly red hair. I waited. Finally, she pronounced her assessment in her soothing voice. "It's your ancestors."

I had called Vanessa because I now felt rooted enough to focus on a trouble area I'd been avoiding for a really long time: my finances. In addition to the student loan I was still dragging around, I now had a few grand of credit card debt that I had racked up since I quit my full-time job.

But the real problem was that I had very little *savings*, a fact made more glaring when you considered that I had been working since I was a teenager. By far, though, my biggest financial block was that I was a chronic undercharger, consistently giving away too much of my time and talents for free—or close to it.

A money healing was due, but my newly honed Ser kept telling me that I needed to look back before I could move forward. So I reached out to ask Vanessa if she did family healings to remove money blocks.

Vanessa suggested a money cleansing. She explained that sometimes when people are having troubles, it could be caused by old ancestral traumas and inherited stories.

Whatever the cause, I was ready to be cured, and soon Vanessa started our hypnosis session by inviting all my ancestors, spirits, and guides to join us. I was lying down on a yoga mat and focusing hazily on a spot on the wall, while she soothingly told me, "I'm going to count backward from five, and with each number, you're letting go . . . and you're letting go."

Then she asked, "Robyn, do you sense any ancestral energies?"

"Yes," I replied.

"How many?" she asked.

"There are three," I answered.

She asked the first one to step forward, and an image of an old woman popped into my head. "What is the name?" Vanessa asked.

Without even thinking, I replied, "Mona."

"What does Mona want you to know?"

I paused, trying to listen. In my mind, I could see an old woman sitting on the ground asking for money. No one looked into her beautiful brown eyes or sat down next to her. I felt Mona's deep loneliness; she didn't seem to have any family or friends to take care of her. I could feel her sadness as well as her fear. Then I said to Vanessa, "Mona is telling me to be safe and to never abandon myself."

Vanessa told me it was time to let her go, and we imagined Mona physically leaving my body, exiting through my feet and onto an illuminated path, where we sent her lovingly into the light.

"You're doing great, Robyn," Vanessa said gently. Then she asked the second ancestral energy to come forward. Immediately, I felt a presence. I couldn't see her face, but she seemed younger than Mona, around forty years old. Vanessa asked for a name. "Carolina" popped into my head. I got an image of Carolina standing on a big property; she was a landowner.

"What does Carolina want to say to you?" she asked.

"She's telling me, 'Don't make the same mistakes we did. Remember what's important. We lived this so you don't have to.'" When Vanessa asked me to elaborate, I told her I saw that money caused Carolina problems with her family. I saw trouble with a brother she was once close to, and I saw the sadness of her husband and daughters. I think they had to leave their home. This vision felt heavy, and I was overcome with pity for Carolina as we sent her into the light.

After I settled back into my breath, we were ready to go in for number three, and Dulce popped into my head. Beautiful Dulce made me tear up. She was a young woman who exuded unfulfilled potential. It seemed that Dulce lived at a time when women's roles were limited, but I could feel the uncontainable yearning to be more. Her message was, "Don't let them hold you back! Do it all! Be it all! Live it all! Do it *now*. Do it for me, for us."

After Dulce left, Vanessa performed Reiki over my body, and I could feel a relaxation in my shoulders as if I was dropping a burden. When we were done, Vanessa told me to drink lots of water and light another candle for my friends' journeys back home.

Later that week, after dropping the girls off at school, I checked my email to find a query from someone at a fitness apparel brand. The company was putting together a panel for Hispanic Heritage Month, and they wanted me to be a part of it. The other confirmed panelists included a high-profile fashion influencer with a zillion followers, an actress on a popular TV show, and a CEO and founder of a tech company.

Feeling honored and slightly unworthy, I scheduled a call to get more info.

"How much?" asked Lars over lunch, always getting straight to the point.

"No pay," I said, stuffing a bite of salad into my mouth and trying to avoid his gaze. To be fair, Lars was giving me a hard time because I had *just* asked him to help me keep my promise of not working for free.

"But this is prestigious!" I wailed. "I just read about the CEO in *Forbes*!"

"Well, *she* can afford to do things for free." Lars said this so matter-of-factly I wanted to stick his face in the salad spinner.

"It's only a few hours of my time, and they're sending me a car. Plus, we get a bunch of fitness gear!" I was trying to convince Lars as much as myself.

"You're working for yoga pants?" replied Lars. "Why don't you just ask them for a fee? You always tell me how much work these panels turn out to be."

I knew Lars was right, but I didn't want to hear it, so instead I looked out the window at the grass that still hadn't been cut.

Needing some air, I took a walk in the woods and switched my mind to trying to figure out who Mona, Carolina, and Dulce were. I didn't know whether they were ancient relatives or my own past lives or maybe just archetypes that represented different parts of myself. But whoever they were, they felt real.

Mona was a beggar, settling for scraps. Carolina was a cautionary tale of what can happen when money goes bad among family. And Dulce was unnurtured talent. Never allowed to shine, she represented unexpressed art, unfulfilled dreams, and an unused voice.

I realized I would need to sit with each of these paradigms.

Contemplating Mona further, she embodied the way I had felt at times with money—making do with what I was handed. I had never been a tough negotiator, even though I knew through articles—some I'd written myself!—that accepting any first offer can cost you hundreds and thousands of dollars over a lifetime. But when I thought of Lars's very logical suggestion that I ask for a fee, it made me cringe.

As I sat beside my favorite stream, a memory sprung loose. I was a teenager, and my mom made me go back into the grocery store to complain because they had overcharged me for something. I'd had a crush on the checkout boy and was livid at the suggestion that I demand a $1.25 refund. I still remember how embarrassed I felt handing him my receipt.

Sitting here now though, thumbing the jagged edges of a rock I'd picked up, I thought about my mom. I began to see that underneath that teenage embarrassment of having to walk into that store to ask for that dollar back was shame because we really needed that money. And under that shame was heartache because the reason was that my father was dead.

I hated that fucking dollar.

And yet I needed those damn dollars, especially if I wanted to travel to Mexico for a group healing.

"Fuuuucccck!" I yelled into the wind as I walked back home to call someone who had no problem demanding money.

"It's not just you, mija!" said my friend Nely in her raspy voice when I confessed my challenge negotiating.

Nely was the founder of a movement called Self-Made, which helps women become entrepreneurs and "rich in every way."

I knew that I needed to clear this block, not just for me but for my daughters. I would be damned if they grew up with the same limits and lack I felt.

"We are not in the American narrative," said Nely. "No one talks about American Latino history. We are the number one minority group in America, but we don't exist! How can we speak up when we don't have a voice?"

"So what do we do, Nely!?" I asked in desperation.

"You have to do the opposite of your feelings—override the computer."

After Nely was president of entertainment at Telemundo, but before she became a *New York Times* best-selling author, she took a break to get her PhD in psychology. When I'd asked her why psychology, she'd said, "So I could understand and heal myself and the toxic masculinity I experienced with my colleagues and partners."

Yet even now, she shared that she sometimes still found herself reverting back to old, scarcity behaviors. "That's when I take action contrary to my damage."

"Take action contrary to your damage."

This sounded like a mantra for money—and my life.

After I hung up with Nely, I emailed the fitness brand inquiring about a panelist fee, explaining how much work and prep and time actually went into these things.

They emailed me back right away, informing me that while they valued my talents, they just didn't have a budget. But they'd keep me in mind for paid consultancy work.

My susto was yelling at me: "Just do it!" "You could make a great connection!" "Do it for the yoga clothes!" But I took action contrary to my damage and wrote them back, thanking them sincerely but letting them know that I wouldn't be able to do the panel. Then I hit send.

I sat back in my chair, feeling exhilarated and kind of nauseous at the same time. Maybe this was what overriding the system felt like?

In my Curanderismo practice, I had been seeing people for free because I was new and needed the practice. But it was still a lot of work that took my whole heart, presence, and energy. So when the next person asked me how much I charged, I let them know I had a "suggested energy exchange" of fifty dollars, but they could pay what they wanted.

Soon, I received a money transfer of fifty dollars with a note saying, "Energy exchange for an amazing limpia!" And just like that, I became a paid curandera practitioner. Curiously, I noticed that once I started charging, people started showing up on time. The exchange made them value our time together, and their investment, more. And I felt more legit and responsible. We were honoring each other and the medicina.

Starting to feel pumped, I called Paloma to tell her about Mexico. "I think I'm going to Costa Rica in January," she said right away, completely ignoring my master plan.

"What the fuck, dude?" I blurted out, despite my intent to stay calm and persuade. "I need your help! I'm worried about Apolonia, she's been weirdly MIA lately, and it would be nice to really see how Lety is doing. And we *all* have our shit to work out. It will be good!" I pleaded.

"I work hard, and I want to have fun on vacation," she replied, "not sit around and talk about my feelings or what's wrong with everyone. I already know what's wrong with everyone."

"Okay."

"And who's paying for this trip, anyway? I pay for everything. It's your turn!" she yelled at me just before she hung up.

It was clearly time to turn my thoughts to Carolina, the second entity, who represented money and family. After that vivid memory of the grocery store came up, more episodes from that time in my life began to surface.

Right after my dad died, we moved into a giant new house that he had built for us in a different part of town. And every morning on the drive to school, my mom would grip the steering wheel, stare straight through the windscreen, and tell me without looking at me that we might have to move again. We had just moved, and I was still struggling to find my way at this wealthier and whiter school. But being my mom, she'd offer no further information.

So I'd just mutter, "Okay," and get out of the car, finding no relief as I walked nervously into the jaws of my new ginormous school.

I would come to find out that the reason my mom was so sad and stressed was because my father had left us this new house but had gone into debt to make it happen for us. In reality there was no money left to afford the taxes or mortgage, and we eventually had to sell the dream house. It was the very last time my mom, sisters, and I lived together under one roof.

My mom told me years later how dedicated my dad had been, looking over sketches and plans from his hospital bed. My mom felt building the house gave him hope and purpose during his terminal illness, and completing it became everything to him in his final months. Leaving it shattered our hearts.

Needing some air, I went outside to find Lars building new fencing for the garden, which I didn't think we needed. Meanwhile, the yard looked worse than ever because Lars had been cutting the lawn section by section with his dinky-ass lawnmower, leaving it uneven, like a patchy beard, not the groomed manicured pumpkin patch I was envisioning, and Astrid's party was this weekend!

Fuming, I walked over to my neighbors' to borrow a regular lawnmower, but it wouldn't cut because the grass was so damn long and wet from the rain. I was so mad I pushed the lawnmower into the garage.

After dinner, while the kids were playing in the living room, I came out and asked Lars point-blank, "Why won't you cut the grass like I asked you? Why don't you listen to me?"

"Why are we spending so much money on a four-year-old's party?"

Ahhhhh. That was what we were fighting about. Money. I saw red.

"Look," I nearly spat at him, "you can't have it both ways. You hated that I worked in the city and was manic mommy and always gone, but now you hate that I'm not bringing in the big bucks. I know you think I'm just hanging out all day, lighting incense and picking flowers and planning parties, but I am healing and writing and putting myself back together again! So if you want a sane and healthy wife and a good mom to those little girls who deserve that, then you will help me. Help me!"

Lucia and Astrid walked in. They looked at us, and Lucia made a motion for me to zip it across her little mouth. She was so sweet.

Only six years old and already trying to play the peacemaker, just like me. But I didn't want to teach her to shut your mouth and stuff your feelings when things around you were on fire. I had lost myself trying to please everyone else, and I just couldn't do it anymore.

"Do you hear me?" I said to Lars, wishing so much to be heard.

Later in the week, still feeling agitated, I reached out to my comadre Linda to talk about savings. Linda ran a financial company that helps BIPOC learn how to invest in the stock market. But a huge part of her work was first helping to heal her clients' money wounds. Overburdened with mine, I reached out.

"I get it!" she said after I shared about my dismal savings and my mom's declaration that "we're poor and we'll always be poor."

"My mom cleaned houses," she said, sharing her own money story. "And I had these wealthy friends who lived in Laguna Beach. I could see the disparity. I thought: 'This is what they get, and this is what we get.'"

Oof, I felt that.

"So how did you change?" I asked, ready for the answer that would make all my money problems disappear.

"I had to first understand the past traumas that led our families to believe that we would always be poor. Everything that had been taken from us in the past, how we had to fight to survive, to labor for every dollar we earned."

I felt like this whole journey had been about taking back all that we had lost.

"I used to think it was my fault," continued Linda. "That there must be something wrong with my family that we couldn't have money. But then I understood that it wasn't that I couldn't amass wealth or make it grow; it was that I *believed* I couldn't. I had this layer of belief that I didn't deserve it. That's when I understood that no one could determine my worth. It didn't matter that my father was alcoholic, that my mom was schizophrenic and bipolar, that I was a teen mom. There was one thing that mattered, and that was the present and what I believed about myself."

"Holy fuck," I said, blown away.

"And once I got clear on my thinking," she continued, "I had to get clear in my finances. I had to clean up my credit report and start learning about investments, and it was scary. I thought I was bad at math!" She laughed.

"I hate math!"

"It's not always easy," she conceded. "But I think of the future, and that inspires me. My parents couldn't think about the future because their day-to-day needs were so great. But I'm playing the long game for my kids. And there is no greater security than trusting and believing in yourself."

After we hung up, I went to sit outside, so grateful to my comadres Nely and Linda for sharing their stories and truth.

Sitting there, I looked at the yard, long in some spots and short in others.

In the big house my dad built us, we didn't have grass. They ran out of money, and it never got landscaped. So outside we had patches of grass and patches of dirt. It was like this—uneven, underresourced.

Underresourced had been the theme of my life. I had even written a lifestyle book about budget living. I had made being poor yet resourceful part of my identity. "When life gives you lemons!" was my unofficial motto. But I was tired of lemons. Of being handed lemons and accepting lemons.

And I had never been handed a bigger lemon than when I worked at my last job. Although our company had been struggling, like most of the media industry, it was when we really began to spiral that I got promoted to leadership, which led to a short but stressful stint that shattered my confidence and burnt me out.

"Why did I take that job?" I had been asking myself since I left. And now with some distance and the help of Curanderismo, I began to understand that I had been working from susto and not my Ser. My Ser knew it was a bad move to take that position; all the signs were there. But my susto had kicked in because the situation looked so much like what I was used to:

- It was something I cared deeply about.
- It was hyperdysfunctional (like my family).
- It was in dire need—cue the savior.

I was not alone in this. There is a phenomenon called the glass cliff in which "women and/or people of color are moved into leadership positions when times are tough, or the organization is in crisis."[1] Meaning when we finally get our shot, instead of getting to lead, we have to save. And trying to save the unsavable was my go-to susto response.

After dinner that night, I apologized to Lars. He came to hug me, and I cried into his chest.

"I'm sorry too," he said. "I just get frustrated because you say one thing but do another. You keep telling me you don't want to work for free, but then you work for yoga pants!"

"Yoga pants are expensive!" I said, laughing. "And I told them no."

"Then you say you want to save money," he continued, "but then you spend so much on a four-year-old's party!" I was about to protest when he interrupted me. "Hold on! Look, I'm not a good talker like you, but I'm just trying to help you like you've asked me to. I'm in this project *with* you; we all are. I don't care about the money, but I do care when you say this healing time is important to you. But you don't treat it that way by taking free gigs when you could be doing your Curanderismo or overspending on a birthday party when you could be buying a plane ticket to Mexico."

He was right. A thirteen-year-old part of me was irritated with Lars just as I had been pissed at my mom all those years ago for making me go back for the dollar. But my adult self could see that they were trying to help me stand up for myself. Lars wasn't trying to patronize me, and my mom wasn't trying to punish me; they were both trying to protect me. We protect what we value, and we value what we love.

I took a deep breath and uttered seven words I had never said in my seven-year marriage. "Can we go over our finances today?"

A few hours later, sitting side by side at our wooden table, I pulled up the Excel file Lars had created, and we looked everything over: fixed costs, as well as variable things like holiday spending and my upcoming Mexico trip. I opened a separate tab to my online banking and showed him what I had in my account. I had never, ever done this in our entire marriage. Lars was a coder by trade, he worked in systems, and he felt safest when he had all the information. I had earned and spent my own money at my own leisure, not always telling him where my money went. I'd been secretive. And that wasn't cool.

No wonder he'd been so on edge.

When I was growing up, my mom never talked about money or finances. She might not have known how, or she might have wanted to shield us from the enormity of her problems. But as scary as it was for me to look at my finances head-on, I knew I was overriding systems and stories that said I couldn't do this, that I was bad at math, and the ugliest untruth of all that whispered, "You're gonna lose it."

Overall, our money situation looked manageable, but barely. I could see in black-and-white how my income projections were lower than I budgeted and my spending higher. For the holidays, we would keep things lean. But now I knew, so I wouldn't blindly overspend. We usually took a beach trip in the summer with friends, and we wouldn't be able to. In the past, I would have plowed through, overcommitted ourselves, and declared I would "figure it out later."

But I knew now that this lack of clarity, this murkiness, was a dangerous playground for my sustos. I had to make changes—for myself and my family.

"Comadre," I told Virginia on Zoom, "I'm gonna have to take a break from our apprenticeship."

She stayed quiet as I explained all my financial and work sustos and how I needed to earn more money.

"It's too much, comadre," I said. "I don't think I'm meant to be a curandera. I'm gonna quit."

"Comadre," she said. "Curanderismo isn't a job. It's a way of life."

"I can't do it!"

"Comadre, you are doing it! We all have our sustos, we all have our shadow, we all have our shit! The work of the curandera is to try to figure out who you are, *all of you*," she said. "Do you know the number one lesson in being a curandera? It's your self-importance."

"Self-importance?" I asked, confused.

"It's not about grandiosity or money or ego," Virginia continued. "A curandera must take care of herself first to do the work. Remember your fifty-two percent." In her book *Woman Who Glows in the Dark*, Virginia's teacher Elena Avila described how the Mexica were master numerologists and had equations for health and happiness, all equaling 100 percent. Fifty-two percent was always the biggest and most important portion of an equation. Virginia was saying that for curanderas, our first 52 percent must be spent on our own healing.

"People think Curanderismo is about healing others, but it's not," she said. "Curanderismo is about healing yourself in order to help others."

I exhaled.

"You really want to 'break cycles' and 'heal generations' and do better for your kids and accomplish all the things you've told me that are important to you?"

I nodded.

"Then don't just say it, comadre; do it."

"*¡Para lograr una sonrisa deslumbrante es necesario usar productos como la pasta dental* 'Shine Bright!' *con peróxido de hidrógeno!*"

"Robyn, that was great!" yelled a producer. "But can you put the emphasis on the first part of the word *hidrógeno?* Thanks!"

"Sure!" I yelled back, gripping the tube of "ultra-white" toothpaste tightly.

I took my maestra's words to heart, and the first thing I did after we spoke was hustle up a new, well-paying freelance gig.

A long time before I was a media boss, I was a TV host and spokesperson. I'd go on morning shows and share Halloween costume ideas for dogs and hosting tips for Super Bowl parties. I'd mostly retired from TV, but I found a toothpaste company was looking for a bilingual spokesperson. I felt weirdly shy to be putting myself out there again in this way, but after looking at the black-and-white of my financials, I knew I needed the money. Inspired by my money *madrinas*, I negotiated the fee at double the offered rate because it was a bilingual job. And they agreed.

I also thanked Rita but said I couldn't afford to fly my sisters and mom to Mexico. Instead, Virginia would do the group healing. She lived in New Mexico, so my sisters and mom could drive from Texas, and Paloma and I could fly in. Virginia even said we could all stay with her. I had found a way to hold the group soul retrieval without wiping out my savings. I was not underresourced; I was being resourceful. Virginia did have one suggestion/condition. Everyone at the soul retrieval had to be there of their own accord. They had to want to go. I couldn't force them.

Feeling more peaceful, I thought about the last money persona, Dulce, who symbolized unrealized potential. I thought of my own dreams of being a curandera and a writer. As a journalist, I'd always written about other people's lives, but maybe it was time to write about my own.

On the morning of Astrid's birthday, I took the girls to pick up the birthday cake and balloons, and when I got home, Lars had cut the

grass. Before I knew it, guests had arrived, and soon we were playing games, eating cake, and hitting the piñata. I was sitting in the
yard watching Astrid and Lucia run around with their friends when
I thought about my dad's building us that big dream house all those
years ago. Ultimately, it didn't matter that we lost it. What was bigger was my dad's love for us, and his deathbed clarity that we
deserved everything, every spectacular thing this magnificent life
had to offer.

Get Rooted Practice #10
Honor Your 52 Percent

As I learned from my comadres Nely and Linda, many of us BIPOC are still feeling the financial consequences of the legacies of colonization and institutionalized racism. It's important to know our histories so we can understand what has happened in our communities. As you saw in this chapter, I began to break cycles by practicing limpia on old, inherited scarcity thoughts and by fighting my own fears around financial literacy and what it means to have abundance. I am still on my money healing journey, but the lesson I take most to heart is one from my maestra Virginia, who taught me about self-importance and honoring my 52 percent.

Although this wisdom was given to me in the context of Curanderismo, honoring our own 52 percent is something we can all benefit from. We practice our self-importance by valuing our time, our talents, our dreams, and ourselves.

Make a list of ways you can honor your 52 percent. It might look like this:

Asking for a raise
Delegating more of your work to a colleague or employee
Taking a day off for self-care
Enrolling in a writing class, or another area, to nurture your don

Write down ways you can begin to honor your time and gifts, and begin to feel how self-importance turns from a phrase into a new way of life. If you feel resistance, ask yourself whether your continued feeling of sacrifice is warranted.

Sacrifice was a word we heard from our families growing up. We heard stories of our parents and ancestors sacrificing so many things: money, dreams, their homelands, language, and ways of being, all so we could continue and prosper.

But at what point do we stop sacrificing? At what point do we ever actually arrive? When do we feel safe enough and complete and worthy enough to reap the benefits and reclaim the rewards of all that sacrificing before us? And what if, throughout all these generations, we had given away too much?

A true way to honor the sacrifices of our ancestors is by taking care of ourselves and honoring and nurturing ourselves in ways they never could. Because if we feel ourselves worthy of sacrifice, then we should feel equally worthy of self-importance and self-respect.

9

Coming Back to Your Body

"Dance with me!" my mom pleaded as she placed her hands on my hips, trying to get me to move to the salsa beat that was blasting from the kitchen radio. I was ten years old and just trying to grab a snack when I found my mom dancing alone in front of the sink.

Ignoring her, with a book in hand, I made a beeline for the fridge while she shimmied in front of my destination, playfully trying to get me to join her.

"Mooooomm!" I wailed. I was a truly terrible dancer; all my sisters made fun of me. But my mom didn't care. When she took me in her arms, I tried not to laugh as she twirled me past the washing machine and pea-green rotary phone that hung from the wall.

"Listen to the beat," she instructed as she tried to get me to move in step with her. "Can't you feel the music?" she asked, letting me go as she swayed rhythmically by herself.

No matter how hard I tried, I could never hear what my mom heard when she was dancing. Instead, I stood by myself, watching her whirl, still listening for the beat that would magically, unbreakably bring me in sync with my mother.

"Whoa, look at that pileated woodpecker!" exclaimed our guide as a gorgeous black bird with a stiff, red gladiator-like crest flew by.

I was on an early-morning hike with a group of middle-aged moms, and all kinds of magic were happening before 7:00 a.m.

After wrestling with my money wounds and tackling my finances, coupled with the realization that my ancestors had sacrificed way too much for me not to savor my one wild and precious life, I was inspired to get out of the world of spreadsheets—and my own head—and do something I had been wanting to do for years: hike.

At the beginning of this journey, I had written down health as an area I had hoped to reclaim. And by trying hiking, I was aiming to reconnect and move my body in ways I'd neglected woefully when I'd been commuting to the city every day.

When I did have time for movement these days, it was usually just a few minutes to pull out my yoga mat before the girls started climbing all over me, thinking I was some sort of human jungle gym. More than just fitness, though, I was seeking some adventure. From my west-facing backyard, I could watch the nearby mountains illuminate at sunset. I knew I was lucky to have such beauty so close by, and with just months now left in this healing journey, I was feeling the urge to seize the day.

I live in a popular hiking town set against a national park. I had first visited the area with Lars and baby Lucia one weekend when we took the train up from the city to hike. We loved it so much that when we became pregnant with Astrid, we decided to move up here. As I was growing up, the flatness of South Texas was my childhood landscape. Now, the stunning beauty of the woods and mountains where we lived astonished me. But once we moved here, I never hiked, ever. Now, the mountains were calling.

Something else was calling too. Long hours spent at my old job meant that I hadn't been able to cultivate any local community. While I would connect with people at parties and such, I rarely had time to go for coffee or yoga or whatever you had to do to develop "grown-up" people friendships. Recently I had found a local hiking club on Facebook—maybe that was the answer.

The group called themselves the Hiking Bandits because it was started by two moms who had to "steal time" to go hiking, usually just before sunrise. They'd walk a trail or climb a mountain, connect with nature, break a sweat, and still have time to come home and get the family dressed, fed, and out the door for school and work. The hikes were usually short—two hours max. But they were long in natural beauty, physical exertion, and, I'd soon find, connection.

"Crow Nest Sunrise Hike! Meet at 5:45 a.m. sharp and bring a headlamp!" read a Facebook post.

When I arrived at my first hike, I was shocked at how well equipped everyone was. It was advertised as an intermediate hike, but I still showed up in sweats, worn-out running shoes, and without a backpack of supplies. Crap!

There was clearly a lot I didn't know yet—for instance, that sometimes hiking really meant rock climbing. My vision of hiking was to slowly walk up a mountain, feeling all meditative and good about myself, taking in the gorgeous vistas. Within five minutes I realized hiking was actually hard as shit. I was huffing and puffing on our entry upward trail as a gray-haired man with walking sticks just breezed on by like a spry mountain goat. I tried making small talk with a friendly woman my age, but I couldn't get any full sentences out because I was breathing so hard. So I just fell quiet and focused on the trail in front of me, which looked endless.

Eventually the group stopped, and I was grateful for the reprieve—for about ninety seconds. We had come to a rocky, vertical section of the mountain called a rock scramble, where you basically cling to the mountain, positioning your feet and hands in crevices to pull yourself up. I paused to stare up the steep mountain face, thinking, "What the fuck did I get myself into?" Then the warm-looking woman whom I had hoped to befriend unhesitatingly started scaling the mountain like some middle-aged Spider-Man. I was seriously considering turning around, but my competitive streak kicked in. "You can do this!" I said to myself. I'd always been active. I used to teach yoga, and I ran a marathon at some point in my life. But this mountain was making me use my body in ways I hadn't in a really long time—or ever. Ignoring my low-key fear of heights and my screaming, underused quads, I pulled and positioned and hoisted my way up.

Mercifully, we soon reached the top, and thankfully it was downright stunning, or I might have pitched our peppy guide right over the edge. From this height, we had a 180-degree aerial view of the Hudson River snaking through the small mountains in the distance. It took what little breath I had away.

I was feeling relieved knowing the last part of the hike was all downhill. But my satisfaction was short-lived when I found it to be a landmine of wet, slippery slick leaves. "Step on the rocks!" our guide yelled—just as I fell on my ass.

The nice Spider-Man lady came over and helped me up as I rubbed my sore butt and grabbed her hand gratefully, then hobbled humbly down the mountain.

"Mama, I think that lady knows you," said Lucia, grabbing my hand on the school playground a few days later. I looked over, and sure enough, a woman dressed like a really groovy mom from the '70s in flared jeans and a turtleneck sweater was waving frantically at me. I almost turned around to see whether she meant to motion to me when she came bounding over.

"Hi! I'm Charlie, from the hike the other day!"

"Ahhh, I didn't recognize you!" It was friendly Spider-lady.

"Are those your kids?" she said, pointing to Lucia and Astrid, who were now on the swings with two other little girls.

"Yeah!"

"Those are mine!" She pointed to the two cute brown-haired girls swinging next to them. "We just moved here from Brooklyn!"

"Us too!" I said. "Well, we actually moved up from Manhattan a few years ago, but I just left my job, so everything is feeling new these days." I was not sure what I was even saying.

Charlie looked unfazed and shared that she used to be a singer in a folk band but was now trying to figure out her "second act."

I nodded in solidarity and then made her laugh by recounting my hiking adventure of falling down the mountain.

"You did amazing for hiking that trail your first time. It's a hard one!" she said. "We're gonna do Devil's Ridge this weekend. Wanna come?"

Devil's Ridge is an advanced hike and the most popular climb in our area. Tourists flooded the mountain on the weekends, lured by amazing photos friends had posted. Often people came unprepared for the challenging terrain without proper shoes, maps, enough water, or the skill set, and endless emergency calls were made to come get people who got lost, sprained their ankles, or worse.

"I . . . I, uh . . . I don't think I'm ready," I said honestly.

"No worries," Charlie said as we walked toward our kids on the swings. "We're going again at the end of the month. Come with us!"

"I'll think about it," I replied, not sure I was up for the challenge.

"Nel-tee-lees-tlee," I pronounced slowly, sounding out a Nahuatl word that was awakening my tongue.

I had come across *neltilitzli* after googling "Aztec words for happiness," because I had joy on my mind. After just a few hikes with the Bandits, I was feeling happier and more energetic than I had in months. When I shared this with Tara, our guide, she told me that hiking was a happiness hack because it released four feel-good chemicals: dopamine, oxytocin, serotonin, and endorphins. I looked this up later and found that it works like this: the dopamine rushed in after completing a task like summiting a mountain; serotonin served as a mood stabilizer that kicked in when in nature; oxytocin, "the love hormone," flowed when connecting with others, which is why it was extra fun to hike as a group; and endorphins are released with physical exertion.

I was feeling the good vibes from all of these, and it got me curious about the ancient ways of happiness. Doing research online, I found an intriguing article from a philosophy professor that contended that because the Mexica believed in the inherent slippery slickness of life, instead of looking for what we would call happiness, they instead sought neltilitzli, a Nahuatl word that meant "well-rootedness." And according to this text, the Mexica rooted down on this slippery slick terrain of life in four foundational ways.

The first way was to root into our physical body. The Mexica were purported to exercise every day, and I had felt myself drop down from my spinning mind into my aching body when hiking. The second way was by maintaining emotional balance, keeping equilibrium between the passions of our heart and the reasoning of our mind. A third path to rootedness was found in community and our place in it. And the final path to rootedness was to appreciate and contemplate the sacred energy that lives in everything.

"Neltilitzli," I breathed out, watching a falling leaf that was floating outside my window. Thinking about sacred connection, I realized that there was one relationship I was really missing, a person I'd been thinking about a lot lately. And so I reached out.

"How are you doing, Mama?"

These last years, I could see the pleasure of life draining out of my mom, with all her worries about her kids. After feeling the happiness hormones flowing back through my body, I wanted to spread some of this joy to her. I knew I'd never get my mom on the hiking trail, but if there was one thing that brought her consistent delight, it was dancing.

My mom had been an accomplished dancer when she was young and had entertained dreams of joining a professional dance troupe and touring the world. My aunts would always tell stories of my mom as a young girl standing in front of the TV and dancing along to Dick Clark and *American Bandstand*. She'd beg her sisters to dance with her, just as she'd pleaded with us kids to dance with her later in life. In high school she was the captain of her dance team, and her girlfriends would cram into my grandparents' small living room as my mom taught her teammates the choreographed routines she'd created.

In college she joined a ballet folklorico group that danced regional dances from Mexico and showcased the Indigenous, African, Spanish, and myriad other influences of the country. She stomped her feet and moved her skirt in a rhythm that was ancestral and enthralling. When she was eighteen years old—one year before she married my dad and had Lety—she auditioned for a touring performance of *Carmen* and beat out dozens of young women to be cast as a flamenco dancer for the opera, which was set in Seville.

The art of flamenco is physically demanding and requires advanced technical skill, so my mom practiced every day for her role with a renowned local flamenco teacher. She excelled in *Carmen*; her whole family went to watch her perform, and the troupe asked her to go on a summer tour with them. She'd get to travel all over the country. My mom was ecstatic; this could be her chance! But then my grandfather forbade her to go. She was too young and unmarried. She wasn't allowed to travel by herself.

So my mom didn't go on the tour, and the next year, she got married and had the first of four babies. When I'd ask her again and again why she didn't just run away and follow her dreams, she'd shrug and shake her head and say, "If I did, maybe I wouldn't have had you."

Hiking had me thinking about the paths we take and the ones we don't. Standing in this midstream of my life, I could clearly see the places I had turned left when I should have gone right. Now, I was just trying to find my way home. And I yearned to be on the same path with my mom again, to know her and have her know me.

And what I most knew about my mom right now was that she had stopped dancing. So I came up with a plan: I would ask my mom to give us dance lessons virtually. It felt like a good way to get her back on the dance floor and a way to connect her to the granddaughters she didn't get to see enough of.

I wasn't sure she'd be up for it, but when I called her, she surprisingly and instantly agreed. Her husband, Ramiro—Ram for short—was also a former dance teacher, and he wanted to help too.

One Sunday afternoon, Lars, Lucia, Astrid, and I gathered in the living room, pushed all the furniture aside, and FaceTimed my mom.

Lars and I both really like old country music, and at our wedding we'd two-stepped our first dance, so we decided the Texas Two Step would be a good place to start. A two-step's beat is slow-slow, quick-quick, to which you kind of slide.

To get in position, I embraced Lars closely, and as we began shuffling around our tight living room, it became quickly apparent that Lars was 10,000 percent better at two-stepping than I was. I could not keep the beat; I couldn't even hear it!

Looking up at Lars admiringly, I complimented him on his dancing prowess, and he told me that when he was a kid, his father had made him and his brothers take foxtrot lessons. My stepdad yelled out from FaceTime that the two-step was derived from the foxtrot. Who knew? And who knew Lars had taken dance lessons as a kid? All kinds of things were being revealed on our makeshift dance floor!

Thankfully, Lucia and Astrid didn't care about my shaky performance. They laughed and danced together and ran in between us. My mom instructed Lars and me to dance super close, with his knee between my legs, and yelled out that I needed to soften my body and let Lars lead me. So I took a breath and tried to relax my body and let go of my underlying need to control everything.

Dancing was my mother's way of connecting; mine was with words. By relaxing into her world of movement, I felt in sync with the music, Lars, and my mom—a meeting point where words didn't need to be spoken. Lars and I circled the length of our living room without a single misstep. The girls clapped, and I smiled at my mom through the screen, wishing that I could reach out and hug her.

"Anyone heard of yoni eggs?"

I was hiking with my local lady crew, Charlie, Rocio, and Amanda, and we had vaginas on the brain.

Besides Charlie, I'd befriended a vivacious fellow Mexican American named Rocio, who had just moved to town and opened a bike shop with her husband. Soon, Amanda rounded out our fab four. Amanda was in her midforties and had sassy platinum hair, impeccable style, and a spunky daughter named Dakota, whom Lucia loved.

Many times, our group stopped and meditated. Listening to the water flowing in the stream and the birds flying overhead, I felt stress and anxiety releasing with each exhale, leaving me feeling more present and aware. Nature was my religion, and I felt very close to our connected sacred energy on these mountains.

I also felt myself growing close to my new comadres as we chatted about what we were making for dinner or what was troubling us at that moment. On these hikes, I found out Charlie's mother had a rare form of cancer that was affecting her neurological system. She was once a dynamic, beautiful woman, but her illness had damaged her motor skills to the point that Charlie had to feed her. As we navigated our way on the trail, Charlie pondered the potential of her mom moving in with her, a prospect that was both welcome and daunting.

Amanda talked about the stresses of her job. She commuted four hours a day to her office and worked as a graphic designer. Her company kept downsizing, so while she was grateful that she still had a job, she was beyond overwhelmed because she now ran a whole division by herself, something once managed by a team of five.

We talked about everything on these hikes, including sex, children, aging, perimenopause, and mostly what we wanted to do with our lives. We were all in the same midlife spot—transitioning, growing, dealing, and healing—and in our circle on these mountains, we were forming a bond that felt protective and affirming.

"A yogi egg?" I asked Charlie.

"A yo-ni egg!" she replied.

Apparently, Charlie had been experiencing pelvic issues since having her kids, and someone had recommended a yoni egg. She told us that a yoni egg is an egg-shaped crystal or stone, such as jade, rose quartz, or obsidian, that you insert into your yoni, or vagina, to supposedly strengthen your pelvic floor muscles.

"I totally pee myself when I jump on a trampoline!" Amanda said. "So let me know how that egg works out for you."

"Me too!" Rocio and I chimed in, laughing.

"But I'm cheap," Charlie continued as we made our way up a rock scramble.

"Why, chica?" Rocio yelled out from up front.

"Well, my lady charges a hundred dollars for a jade one."

"Damn, girl!" said Amanda as she tried to find her footing in the cracks of the mountain. "That's a light fixture," she huffed. She was in the midst of a home renovation, and all her money—and energy—was tuned to that.

"I know," said Charlie as she sat on a rock. "That's why I went on Amazon and bought three for thirty dollars."

"Your yoni is cheap," I teased Charlie as I sat next to her, taking in the view of the Hudson River, and we all howled in laughter.

"My yoni is priceless!" she responded playfully.

"Okay, we'll all pitch in to buy you the one-hundred-dollar magical jade choncha egg," said Rocio as she picked up a small stone and gently tossed it at her.

We all smiled as we took in the majestic vista. "Here's to our priceless yonis," I said. We took a selfie against the picturesque backdrop. I yelled, "One, two, three: say yoni!"

As I jumped on the trampoline later with the girls—and tried not to pee myself—I thought about how much my body, and life, had changed since I'd had the kids. Lars and I had enjoyed a whirlwind romance and got pregnant and married within a year of meeting. Astrid followed less than two years later, and the year after that, I started the job in the city working at the magazine. It was a fast and furious series of mostly highs and some lows, and now I honestly felt like I was just catching my breath and coming back into my body.

My friend Sara taught restorative yoga, and the advice she gave to her students always stuck with me. "Coming back to our bodies is like reconnecting with an old friend," she'd say. "You have to take the time to catch up and listen and see what's going on."

Hiking and dancing had helped take me out of my head, where I tended to live, and land back in my body, and I was humbled. In my youth, I used to just tell my body what to do, but now I had to listen. It was hard, because there was fear, sadness, grief, and regret in my body. I could feel it in the tightness of my hips, in the aches of my back, in the tension in my shoulders. Walking, and climbing, and dancing, I felt like I was releasing some of that, and it reminded me of years ago when I was first training to be a yoga teacher.

I had started a regular yoga practice after a horrible heartbreak with someone I'd been convinced I would marry. When the relationship ended, I'd been in agony—dumbfounded and confused. I would go to yoga every day to try to get out of my tortured mind, but it followed. And then one day we were trying to get into triangle pose, a harder-than-it-seems position where you have to ground your feet firmly to have the rootedness to grow open and then finally, gloriously, expand your arms.

I was struggling with the pose when my teacher came over and said in a commanding tone, "Robyn, look at your feet, pay attention to your feet! *Love* is attention!" In that moment, I looked down at my feet and really saw them. I noticed how my second toe was longer than my big toe, how flat my feet were, and the bright, sunny blue color of my nail polish. And in that moment, I really saw the girl on the mat with the hopeful blue toes and the blown-open heart, and I cried, finally seeing, and feeling, me.

I found myself getting to know my body again, and she was changing. I had become stiffer with age, hardened with life and sustos, and didn't feel that brazen invincibility or enduring hope

I'd known when I was younger—or even six months ago. I missed that girl and wondered whether she'd ever come back.

"I'm in the hospital" read a text from my mom.

I called her immediately. "Mom! What's going on?" I yelled when she answered.

"I'm okay, I'm okay," she said, sounding tired.

"What happened? Are you hurt?" I asked.

"I had Ram bring me to the ER, because my blood pressure was really high and I felt dizzy, but I'm feeling better. They're gonna release me soon."

"Oh my God, Mom! You need to take care of yourself," I said, trying not to yell at her, even though I wanted to scream. "Are you taking your medicine?"

My mom had had high blood pressure for decades. Once she'd gone to the dentist, and when they conducted the routine blood pressure check, they were so shocked at how high it was that they insisted she go straight to the hospital. She didn't.

"The doctor switched me to something new because the last one was really hard on my kidneys," she said on the phone. "But I think I'm having a bad reaction to this new one, so they prescribed something different. Ram is filling it now; then we can leave. I'm good, I promise! Don't worry!" she said. I could hear the nurses coming in. "I have to go, but I'll call you when I get home." And she hung up.

Looking at the phone, I could feel my own blood pressure begin to boil, because I wanted her to take better care of herself, of her precious body.

My mom was still working even though she had just turned seventy—mostly because she needed to, but also because I don't think she really knew how to slow down. She still did most of the cooking and cleaning at the house, tending to my sister and nephew and stepdad, even though they were all grown up.

I had tried to explain to my mom that she needed to take care of herself and suggested she start walking or take up gardening. But she just listened quietly—confused, as if I was suggesting the world was flat, or responding in the way she had reacted when I told her that Lars didn't like beans: utterly perplexed. Self-care was the antithesis of how she viewed the world, which was to give, give, give. While it made my mom who she was, I was now terrified it was making her sick.

As I was driving later, a memory popped up of a visit I'd had with my mom years before. With all her daughters finally out of the house, my mom had redecorated, and when I visited, she proudly showed me around room by room. Her aesthetic was what an empty nester would create, with lots of doilies and ceramic figurines. It wasn't my style, but she clearly loved it. "It all looks so pretty, Mom."

Standing in one empty room, with the light shining on the paisley pattern of the bedspread, her eyes grew watery, and, unprovoked, she laughed sadly and said, "What's the point?" She gestured around at the hard work she had put into fixing the room. "Why even bother?" In the quiet, my mom's susto popped up and told her accusingly, "What's the point? It's all just gonna fall apart anyway." And that was why she stayed so busy.

Thinking now about that memory from years ago, I wished I had told my mom what I'd been thinking at that moment, which I was just now realizing. "Look at me, Mom! I'm here! I'm your daughter! I'm real! I'm the point."

The next morning at dawn, I met the crew at the Devil's Ridge trailhead, and one by one we began to ascend.

The trail began at sea level, but in less than a quarter of a mile, we had reached an elevation of eleven hundred feet. I was taking it easy, bringing up the rear, knowing slow and steady would help me get where I needed to go. Most of the climb was rock scramble, which required my whole concentration, so I didn't talk much. To avoid hitting any overhanging rocks, I decided not to wear my baseball cap, leaving my view unobstructed. Things were going well until we got to a V-shaped ravine that was slippery smooth.

Tara went first, showing us how to stretch our legs out like a starfish to keep our grip while pulling and hoisting ourselves up. I tried to mimic her, but the center was too slippery. I tried to veer right when Tara yelled out, "Careful!"

Just five feet over was a steep drop. I nodded, showing I understood, and angled back left to the slippery middle. Everyone had made it up but me. "Fuck," I muttered. I felt stuck, and my arms were getting sore gripping on to these tiny cracks in the rock. I wished I hadn't looked over the edge because now I felt fear creeping in.

"You can do this, Robyn!" Charlie yelled from above, and I wanted to cry for some reason.

"Fuck!" I yelled. I didn't feel like I could. I didn't feel like I could do any of this at all.

I was holding on for dear life when Tara yelled, "You have to let go!"

"Did she say 'let go'?" I thought. A part of me did want to let go. To push off and do a back flip straight into the abyss. It was so painful to hold on, wasn't it?

I could hear everyone above me encouraging me and yelling out instructions, but I was frozen. I couldn't even feel my fingers.

"They're gonna have to helicopter me off this mountain," I thought. Then I heard my mom telling me to soften my stance and listen. I breathed calm into the fear flooding my body, and, looking down, I understood what they were shouting. I was gonna have to let go, but just to slide down to a point where I could put my foot on a protruding rock and then hoist myself up again.

"I got it!" I yelled. And I let go, cradling the mountain and sliding down until my foot landed on the ledge.

"Yes!" everyone erupted. From here I could easily see my way up like a ladder. I gave my friends a thumbs-up and, leaning into the mountain, made my way.

As I hoisted myself to the summit, everyone cheered. We all hugged, and I felt electric. I finally felt what my mom had been wanting me to feel all those years when she was dancing: alive.

Gazing down on our town below, I looked in the direction of my house and imagined Lars and the girls nestled inside. I was overcome with such love for them and with the emotion from the hike that tears sprang to my eyes. From this height, I had a full 360-degree view, and I could see in all the directions.

Then I looked up. The golden pink of the rising sun pierced straight into my heart. I instantly remembered huddling with my parents and sisters on a picnic table as we watched the dreamy ombre sunrise at a New Mexican rest stop on our yearly road trip from Texas to California. Looking now at the heavens ablaze, I felt the vastness of a thing that will outlive you and every pain you know. If I could have grabbed it out of the sky and wrapped all of us in it at that moment, I would have.

Later in the week, my mom was feeling better and insisted on continuing with our next FaceTime dance lesson. And this time we chose salsa. We all gathered in the living room, and I cued up Marc Anthony—and instantly the crowd went wild! Lars grabbed me and started doing something that maybe could have been interpreted as the lambada, the forbidden dance of love. Seeing us getting our married-people moves on, my mom turned her sights to the girls, trying to teach them to shimmy their little bodies from side to side like she was doing expertly. Instead, the girls hopped in a circle with their hands in the air, doing some freestyle ballet moves.

Wanting to show us how it's done, my mom and stepdad pulled out some seriously age-defying pro moves that could have gone viral if I posted them. As we salsaed around the living room, we sang aloud to the lyrics: "*¡Voy a reír! ¡Voy a bailar! ¡Vivir mi vida, lalalalá!*" (I'm going to laugh! I'm going to dance! I'm going to live my life, lalalalá!)

I looked at my mom on-screen, we locked eyes, and I saw something I hadn't seen in a long, long time: joy.

Get Rooted Practice #11
The Four Paths to Rootedness

When I first mentioned the four paths to rootedness to my maestra Virginia, she reminded me that *her* teacher, Elena Avila, wrote of a similar four-part equation in her book, referring to the care for an "intact soul." According to Avila, the Aztecs (Mexica) believed that for a person to have a healthy soul, you had to maintain your physical body, feel and balance your emotions, and maintain your mind and your spirit—in that order.

From a Curandersimo perspective and from Mexica philosophy, it's clear that inhabiting our bodies, balancing our emotions, being aware of our thoughts, connecting to community, and communing with Spirit are integral ways to stay rooted. I can also add from my own lived-in-my-body experience that the through line for all these equations and paths is *connection*.

These simple but powerful ways to help us get rooted have become an integral part of my life, and I hope they will for you too. We need all our tools to root down in this slippery slick world, so here I elaborate a little more on each path, or connection point, so you can begin to experience and integrate them into your daily life.

1. Connection to our body: Moving it, being in it, and listening to it connect us to ourselves. In slippery times, most of us go straight to our head: worrying, obsessing, planning. Instead, we can calm the chaos in our mind and root into the steady knowing of our body. By inhabiting our body, we begin to notice how we hold our breath around certain people, how we exhale around others, how our stomachs tighten when we enter certain places, and how somewhere we have never been before can still feel so much like home.

Moving your body regularly is a good way to get rooted, whether you hike a mountain or find your flow while running. Besides fitness, there are myriad ways to reconnect to ourselves, like unwinding with a massage or acupuncture. Warm baths, sweaty dancing, hot sex, and self-pleasure can all do the trick too. The possibilities are endless, and finding what works for you will be part of your path.

2. Connection and balancing our emotions: I tend to hear and listen to my Ser, my right knowing, when I am emotionally balanced and connected. Meditations and spiritual journaling can help us unearth and clear out buried feelings so that we can stay rooted and true to ourselves. Whenever I am feeling overwhelmed, overanxious, overstressed, or just over it, I get the feelings out of my body via a limpia, breath work, meditation, or writing the feeling down on paper. I call this tool "over and out." Remember this the next time you are feeling overwhelmed.

3. Connection to each other as community: Having a place where we can offer support and feel supported is paramount to feeling seen, heard, and loved. Often as women or BIPOC, we are not used to being carried. We have learned from susto and socialization to shoulder the responsibility and carry the burdens ourselves. That is why it is a powerful practice and reframing to ask for the help we need. In circle, we hold each other and are held.

4. Connection to Mother Nature and Spirit: Nature helps connect us to what is bigger so that we feel our right place in the greater whole. Hiking through cathedral-like forests that make you quiet with reverence; floating freely in the buoyant ocean, feeling the universe really does have your back; and chatting with the squawking bird in your backyard who reminds you so much of your favorite aunt—these are all sources of connection that lower stress and increase creativity and joy.

Two organizations I really like that help BIPOC connect with nature are GirlTrek.org, a global movement of over one million Black women that leverages "the historic legacy of walking and the power of self-care as a pathway to heal and transform lives," and Recla.ma, a spiritual wellness community helping women of color reclaim themselves through hiking and journaling.

I created this acronym to help remind you to stay connected:

Remember the body.
Open and release.
Offer yourself to others.
Touch nature.

The biggest lesson I learned about rootedness is not to just think about it but to integrate it, to practice it, to live it. These are paths, ancient and everlasting, to help you find your way, but always above all stay present, stay connected, and root into what is true for you.

PART FOUR

The South: Facing the Fire

10

Following the Hummingbird

"I'll have another drink!"

Paloma, who knew everyone, had a friend who had just moved to our little town, and she and her husband invited us all over for a housewarming party. I wasn't feeling particularly festive, but it was Thanksgiving weekend, and despite the last few stressful days, I still had so much to be grateful for. It was hard to believe that just a year ago, I'd had a miserable Thanksgiving, working the entire holiday weekend while Lars took the girls to get a Christmas tree without me. But I had moved those winds.

The hosts were from Italy, and their house was gorgeous. Though the weather was chilly, we chatted happily around a blazing firepit while the kids chased each other around. After refusing for hours because I was trying really hard not to drink during this healing journey, I finally accepted a glass of red wine. I loved big cabernets, and soon I was pouring myself another, feeling the pressure of the dramatic last few days washing away. At some point, the party moved indoors, and as it neared bedtime, Lars motioned for us to leave.

I knew I should go with him, put the kids to bed, snuggle up, and maybe get busy in front of the fire like the old days. "You can't leave yet!" wailed a neighbor I had just met but who was quickly becoming my new best friend. "Have another drink!" and someone filled my glass. Music floated in from the other room, where people were gathering around the piano.

After days of tension headaches, I just wanted to keep the flying feeling going, so I helped the girls into their coats and gave Lars a kiss. "I'll be home soon, I promise!"

That was the last thing I remembered.

Weeks earlier, after spending so much time connecting with my mom, new friends, and body via hiking and dancing, I kept up the focus on my health by catching up on overdue doctor's appointments. I scheduled myself for the works: a teeth cleaning, a Pap smear, an eye evaluation, and a visit to the dermatologist to have my sunspots checked out.

All was good and uneventful until my gynecologist scheduled me for a mammogram. I've always had fibrous, dense breasts, so I wasn't surprised when, immediately after the mammogram, I was sent to get a sonogram. But as the tech spent an agonizingly long time running her scope over one area again and again, I started to feel uneasy.

It turned out that I had a "suspicious" nodule that needed to be biopsied. The biopsy itself was straightforward and painless. They made a small incision to get the sample, and I was out in an hour with a small ice pack on my chest. Then they let me know I'd get the results back in a week.

A week! How was I supposed to stay cool while waiting so long? Lars assured me it was no big deal and reminded me that I didn't have any family history of breast cancer. Yet one in eight women get it in their lifetime. Would one of those be me?

The next morning I woke in a near panic attack and went to my altar to give myself an egg limpia and light candles to the ancestors for protection. Soon, I felt more soothed, but my mind kept thinking of my dad's cancer, wondering, "Is this how it all starts?" I was sitting quietly at my altar with the light streaming in from the east when my Ser told me to go pray outside.

It was brisk, but the sun was shining, and without thinking, I unbuttoned my nightgown, letting the power of the sun's rays penetrate my chest. The neighbors were probably getting a show, watching their topless hippie neighbor soak in the morning sun, but I didn't give a damn. In that raw moment, I felt connected to everyone everywhere awaiting test results or undergoing a health crisis. As I tenderly brought my hands to my chest, I prayed for a healing for all of us.

In Nahuatl, there is a term for that in-between, neither-here-nor-there feeling: *nepantla*.[1] The word was first recorded by Spanish friars after the conquest and was attributed to an Indigenous man who referred to his present life as in nepantla: no longer under Mexica rule but not fully accustomed to these new European, Catholic ways.[2]

I found myself in that murky nepantla state waiting for the biopsy results. In between healthy and sick, between hurting and healed. After half a year of soul retrievals, I'd felt myself fill out into a more rooted version of myself. But now I could feel the strength of my Ser collapsing.

After four agonizing days of waiting by the phone, I still hadn't heard anything. I felt overwhelmed by the uncertainty of what lay ahead and took to my woods, which, as winter approached, were even more striking in their starkness. With the foliage thinned, tree after tree laid out before me, creating a melancholy path. The river was more accessible now without all the brush, and I could walk right up to it, admiring the cattails holding rooted in the mud. They swayed in the wind, waving at me. Feeling heartbroken but seen, I waved right back.

After meandering for a bit, I ended up on Main Street in front of a bright shop with a stenciled sign that read, "Supplies for Creative Living." Who didn't need supplies for creative living?

"Hi! Is this a new store?" I called out as I entered the sunshine-filled space, crowded with brightly colored journals, pens, and watercolors. I put down my worry while picking up rainbow-patterned origami paper and sniffing the clean, woodsy smell of paper notebooks. After a long chat with the sweet owner, aptly named Grace, I splurged on watercolor pencils and a sketch pad and bought each of the girls a pack of tiny colored pencils I knew they'd love.

At home, I sat in my office and tried to draw Mama Natalia, playing with the pencils that turned to watercolors when you applied a small wet brush. Smearing the lines that I'd drawn felt good, freeing, like I was exploring that spacious in-betweenness. Looking at a photo of Mama Natalia that Dora had sent me, I noticed for the first time that she wore an unusual ring on her wedding finger. Instead of a band, it was four symmetrical pearls. I wondered if it meant anything. Mama Natalia had three children; maybe the fourth pearl was her husband? As I sketched the ring as four small circles, I found myself letting go of trying to grasp the meaning of the ring—to somehow better understand Mama Natalia, or even life itself—and relaxing back into the watercolory nepantla of the moment.

That night, I had a dream so horrible, my cries woke Lars. "Help me, help me! I'm hurt!"

"Babe, are you okay?"

I awoke, and it took me a moment to place myself. "I had the worst dream," I said after realizing I was safe in my bed. "My mom and sisters were all in a car, and my mom was driving," I said, relaying what still felt so real. "We were trying to get home," I continued. "I could see the house, but we were driving on rollercoaster rails, and she lost control, and we toppled down a long distance and crashed. I wasn't bleeding, but I could feel the pain internally. I couldn't find my phone to call 911, and everyone got out of the car and just walked away. I yelled to people passing by, 'Help me, help me! I'm hurt!' but no one paid attention."

"Shh, shh," he said, drawing me into him. "It's not real. You're okay."

"I'm okay, I'm okay," I said to myself, burrowing into Lars's chest. "But am I okay?" I wondered. Why were the test results taking so long? And with only two months left in my healing project, so much was still unresolved. As Lars drifted back to sleep with a gentle snore, I lay there with a scary sense of foreboding. In my dream, no one could see my pain but me. Was no one coming to help?

The next day, I called Lety, craving the comfort of sharing. We chatted for a bit, and I mentioned that I'd decided to travel to Texas right before the holidays, my last-ditch effort to get everyone on board for the soul retrieval.

I told Lety I'd be there for her birthday, which was right before Christmas. She was so happy, I got excited too. I hadn't been home for the holidays in nearly a decade and started rattling off all the things I wanted to do.

"Okay, I want to go by our old house, and I want to have lunch at Dad's ballroom—"

Before I could go on, she cut me off. "They sold the ballroom; it's not a restaurant anymore." After my father died, his event hall was bought and turned into a restaurant. I had never had the desire to go . . . until now.

"It's closed?" I asked, feeling as though I had missed a chance at something.

"It's a funeral home now."

"Oh my God!" So. Ominous.

"And I'm not going by Mariposa," she said, referring to our childhood home. "I used to go by there all the time when I was high," she continued. "I couldn't care less about that place. Remember when we went skiing in Taos? I wanna go *there*. I want to see something nice. I want good memories."

I got where she was coming from—I mostly did, anyway. I wanted us to make good memories again too. I hung up without mentioning my biopsy. The next day, still no word, and I wanted my mommy. I was so relieved when she picked up, and after chatting a bit, I was about to tell her about my biopsy when she started in about Apolonia.

"What's going on, Mom?"

"It's Apolonia. She didn't come home last night."

"Mom, she's a grown woman; just text her. She's probably staying with a friend."

"She's been hanging out with people from *those* apartments down the street, and I don't like it." Near my mom's house were some sketchy apartments where people went to party.

"I don't know what to say, Mom," I replied.

She started complaining about something else. We hung up without me telling her about my biopsy.

"*¡Quédate con lo tuyo!*"

Desperately needing to ground myself, I set up an SOS session with Virginia. Seeing my maestra on Zoom, wearing red and white, with her candles and altar in the background, instantly made me cry. I wished I could crawl through the screen and lay my head in her lap. I filled her in quickly on what was going on with me and was then moving on to my mom and our worries about Apolonia when she cut me off sharply.

"*¡Quédate con lo tuyo, comadre!*" she said. "You need to stay with your own shit!"

When I looked at her, confused, she continued, "You have spent the majority of our time together talking about your family's drama and susto. I know you love them and want to help, but you need to stay with your own healing, comadre! Your body is screaming for your attention! It's trying to tell you something, mija, but you are just . . . not . . . listening." She touched her hand over her left breast, the exact location of my biopsy. I hadn't told her where it was.

"People are our mirrors, comadre," she said, "so before you can help anyone else, you have to focus on your own limpia, your own

healing! Don't abandon yourself to save other people. It's a distrac-
tion. Stay rooted, mija, and clear that shit up!"

She had never talked to me so forcefully, which scared me
because I knew it meant that she was worried. Virginia was intuitive like Mama Natalia, and I wondered what she knew—or could
see—and wasn't telling me. What she *was* telling me though, loud
and clear, was to stay with my own shit. "But what is my body trying to say?" I wondered.

After my platica with Virginia, I took a bath. I had my hands on
my breasts, trying to do healing Reiki, when I realized I was in the
direction of the south now. The direction of the south is the place
of willpower and also of children. It's guarded by the energy
essence Huitzilopochtli, who is also called "the Hummingbird to
the Left."

According to legend, the Mexica were a nomadic people. They
hailed from a mythical place called Aztlán. One day, they received
a message from Huitzilopochtli in the form of a hummingbird.
He told them to travel south, and when they saw an eagle perched
on a cactus eating a snake, that is where they should build their
home. When they saw this vision on an island in Lake Texcoco,
they built the ancient city of Tenochtitlan, now home to Mexico
City. Some believe that the "hummingbird to the left" symbolizes
our hearts, which lie in the south and left of our chests. That is
exactly where my biopsy was. Placing my hand over my heart, I
asked, "What are you trying to tell me? Where are you trying to
lead me?"

"You know what to do" was the answer I heard back.

The morning after the party, I lay in bed, head pounding. I could
hear Lars with the girls downstairs making breakfast. I texted
Paloma. "What happened?"

She immediately called. "You got wasted. I had to walk you
home, and you wouldn't wear your shoes. Do you remember singing 'Volver, Volver' and trying to play the piano?"

I didn't. None of it. The very last thing I remembered was trying to explain susto to someone, but the words weren't coming out right.

Fuck.

"I gotta go," I told Paloma. I splashed my face with cold water and went downstairs to my family eating pancakes.

"Hi," Lars said flatly.

I went to grab coffee, but there was none left. "Mama, did you have fun at the party?" Astrid asked.

"I did!" I said, though I didn't remember.

"What did you do?" Lucia asked.

"Well, let's see. We danced and played the piano, then I walked home."

"What time did you come in?" Lars asked. "I went to sleep with Astrid around midnight because she was crying, and you still weren't home."

"Just after that," I answered, lying reflexively as I looked into my empty coffee cup.

I remembered the very first time I told a lie. I was six, and my dad had an old-fashioned metal fan with exposed blades, and I was mesmerized by it. I used to love stopping and starting the fan to watch the blades whirl faster and faster until I couldn't see them anymore. Once, after I flicked the off switch and the blades were slowing down, I curiously stuck my finger in the fan—and ended up with a nasty, bleeding cut. Crying, I ran to my parents, but when they asked me what happened, I knew I'd get in trouble, so I lied and said I'd cut it swinging from our mailbox. I don't know how that came to me, and my mom wondered aloud how I could possibly get harmed from a mailbox. But my dad believed my lie. He explained to my mom that our metal mailbox was sharp, and it could happen. He then soothed me and tended to the cut I'd inflicted on myself, the shame of my lie worse than my open wound.

After breakfast, the girls watched TV, and I crawled back into bed feeling horrible. I was trying to sleep, hoping I could wake up again and this whole terrible week would be gone, but my eyes refused to close.

Lars came in and sat at the edge of the bed. I looked up at him helplessly. "I know you're worried about your biopsy," he said, "but I didn't enjoy last night."

I nodded but didn't say a word.

"I wanted you to come home with us, me and the kids. To play cards and have fun, but you stayed."

"I'm sorry," I said, touching his arm, trying not to cry.

"Listen," he continued, "I know you don't think I like this project or understand your Curanderismo, but I do like it. Because it's making you different. You're more present. You're with us now, not just next to us on your phone."

"I get it," I started to say.

"Do you?" he asked, looking at me.

"I do," I said, looking back. I really did.

Softening, Lars asked, "Do you need me to ground you?" as he gently laid on top of me. I hugged him hard, but then I felt like throwing up, so I scooched aside and laid my head on his chest.

"I think I've figured out what my car crash dream meant," I said after pushing down a wave of nausea.

"Yeah?" he encouraged gently.

"I'm going to have to save myself."

My biopsy results finally came back; my nodule was benign.

I thanked the doctor and then my ancestors, but I still felt heavy. I knew what my body was trying to tell me. It wasn't that I had cancer. I had an affliction no one could see. One that I had ignored for a really long time.

I first got blackout drunk when I was thirteen years old, just two months after my dad died. My boyfriend invited me to the local carnival. I was so excited; I curled my hair and bought a new sailor top. He was excited too, having saved all his money working weekends in his parents' furniture shop so we could ride all the rides.

It was a balmy spring night, and his older brother got us beers. I had never drunk alcohol before but loved it immediately. I loved how I could drink this effervescent elixir and magically leave my body, and everything else, far behind. I didn't want that feeling to stop, so I kept drinking—until I threw up behind the bumper cars.

I remember my boyfriend being so upset as I heaved out all that Miller Lite and sausage on a stick. "I bought all these tickets!" he said, disappointedly waving the now useless little red stubs in front of me. "I wanted us to have fun and ride the Ferris wheel! But you can't even walk!"

Two things changed in that moment.

I realized I could lose myself in drinking. And I learned to live with disappointing myself.

I didn't want to do either anymore.

After giving Lars the good news about my biopsy, I told him there was something else I needed to share. He listened quietly as I confessed that I drank too much. That for about 90 percent of the time, I was fine: I could pull back, cut myself off, and go home and be a good-ish wife and mom. But for a dangerous 10 percent of the time, I didn't feel like I had control. I gave alcohol the wheel, and just let it take me until I ran out of booze or blacked out—or both. Like my dream, I wasn't bleeding on the outside—not anymore, anyway, thinking back to when I had bled on my dress. But I *was* still hurting on the inside where no one could see. Not because they didn't want to help. But because I lied about it. And I couldn't lie anymore. My body, my brain, and Virginia were saying "quédate con lo tuyo," to stay with myself. Instead of abandoning my broken heart, I should attend to it.

Standing in my kitchen, I told Lars life *was* slippery slick and I couldn't stop that, no matter how hard I worked, how much I tried to help my sisters, or how much I drank. But I could stop *me*. From abandoning myself, from flying away and leaving my soul behind. This soul retrieval couldn't be done with drums, but with a decision. And I was making it. I was going to quit drinking. Not because my life was bad, but because it was good, and I wanted it to stay good.

I finished my rambling soliloquy, and he looked at me for a long minute while I tried to gauge how any of this had landed.

Then he said the three most rooted words I could hear: "I love you."

I called a sober friend, a fellow healer, and the next morning, I walked into a small room of women I didn't know and shared the one thing I did know about myself. "My name is Robyn, and I am an alcoholic."

Get Rooted Practice #12
Hummingbird Meditation

Huitzilopochtli is the guardian of the South and an essence we can call on to help guide us home. Huitzilopochtli is associated with warriorship and the sun, and we can call in this fiery energy—this willpower of the warrior—when we need the strength to fight for ourselves.

So many of us are fighting battles, seen and unseen.

I created this hummingbird meditation so we can call in the potent energy of the hummingbird to help us strengthen our spirit and resolve.

You may want to record yourself reading this meditation and play it back, or visit www.robynmoreno.com/meditation for more meditations.

You would ideally do this meditation around noontime when the sun is at its peak. You can do this outside or in a sunny spot inside your home, in a location that is comfortable for you but where you can also feel the sun's powerful rays.

Sit facing the sun, find a relaxing seat, soften your gaze, and slowly begin to deepen your breathing. Feel the warmth of the sun on the crown of your head, and inhale the strength of the sun, imagining the power of this golden light infusing your spirit and body. Exhale and tilt your head up, feeling the sun's glow on your face. Inhale as the warmth nourishes and enlivens you. Feel the invigorating golden rays as they pour down your neck and shoulders, straight into your chest. Place your right hand over your heart. As you feel its rhythm, imagine with every beat it's sending this vital energy everywhere in your body where you need it.

With your hand over your heart, keeping the base of your palm steady, slowly raise your hand, and bring it down, gently patting over your heart, mimicking a drumbeat.

With every drumbeat over your heart, imagine that you are sending energy throughout your body:

*Beat—Send energy to your mind so you have the clarity to make a
decision.*

Beat—Send strength to your mouth so you can speak your truth.

*Beat—Send love to your tender, beating heart so it knows it's never
alone.*

*Beat—Feel the fire in your belly burn, giving you the will to do the
thing you know you must do.*

*Beat—Feel the strength of your back body, knowing your ancestors
are always pushing you forward.*

*Beat—Feel the fire in your hips and groin, knowing your strength is
ancestral and is connected to a fire that never stops burning.*

*Beat—Send courage to your legs and feet so you can stand up for
yourself as a warrior, a* guerrera, *a protector of your own precious
heart.*

Place your left palm over your right hand, cradling your heart.

And now you do the hardest part, the bravest thing: you listen to
the hummingbird in your heart. What is it telling you? What is the
message it has for you?

When you feel you are done, bow your head and give thanks to
this mighty hummingbird energy, and promise to keep connecting
and listening to this warrior inside who will help guide you back
home.

11

Home Sweet Home

"You might want to get some holy water."

I was headed to San Antonio for a long weekend and felt as though I was preparing to do battle with the devil. I had reached out to Virginia because, while in Texas, I wanted to spiritually cleanse my mom's house of the layers of susto she'd accumulated over the years like a heavy fog. In the back of my mind, I also had the idea that I'd be able to convince my mom, Lety, and Apolonia to do a soul retrieval with me. I had hoped to bring Lars and the girls down with me, but my Ser told me this was a trip I should take alone.

To do the house limpia, Virginia instructed me to open all the cabinets and curtains in my mom's home and walk room to room with copal burning while reciting a prayer—paying special attention to the corners of the room where energy can get trapped. "Weird stuff might happen," she warned me. "When I cleansed my mom's house after she died, doors kept slamming shut."

Weeks into my new sobriety, I wasn't sure that heading down to see my family—with all their steady drama and sustos—was the best idea. But I had less than two months to go until my healing project ended, and I was determined to cross the finish line.

Once I landed in San Antonio, I grabbed my forgettable rental car and drove to my mom's house. It was only twelve minutes from the airport, but I always got lost. I didn't have a natural homing device for her place—probably because it has never felt like *home* to me. After we had to sell the house our dad built for us, we all scattered, and eventually, my mom bought this house on a street called Starlight, a name that felt taunting because there didn't seem to be any magic or joy there now.

As I pulled in, I saw her house looked the same, but weathering had chipped the paint's facade.

My mom came out to greet me before I even stopped the engine.

"Hi, Mama!" I said, stepping out and giving her a hug. My mom was tiny, but I felt she had shrunk even more. "Is Apolonia inside? I want to say hi."

I followed her through the front door, and though it was light outside, all the blinds were drawn, creating a cave-like darkness.

I greeted my stepdad in the kitchen, which was the brightest spot in the house. While we were talking, my twenty-five-year-old nephew came in to give me a hug. Apolonia had Jacob young, and my mom had helped raise him. He was a tender soul and such a bright spot in our lives. He was on his way to his overnight shift as a baggage handler at the airport. During the holidays, he was working fifteen-hour days.

After he left, my mom went to knock on Apolonia's door. "Robyn's here. Come say hello."

And soon my little sister came out.

I gave her a hug. "Hi, mama. It's good to see you. How have you been?" She was wearing pajamas and no makeup. She looked so young and vulnerable.

"I'm okay," she said slowly, exuding not-okayness.

"We're about to go to dinner. Do you want to come with us?" I asked.

"No, I'm good. I'm gonna rest," she said.

"Okay, babe. I'm here all weekend, so I'll catch up with you."

The last time I was in town, I told her I would pick her up and take her out to eat, but I never came back for her. I wanted to take her with me this time.

Forty-five minutes later, we met Lety and her husband, Cesar, at a hip Mexican restaurant. Usually I would have ordered a fancy silver margarita at the bar as we waited for them, but instead I ordered a Topo Chico mineral water with lime. As my mom and I watched the crowd, I felt good. I hadn't had a drink in twenty-one days, and so far I was feeling rooted in my new sobriety. The festive holiday atmosphere was contagious, and I was happy to be here with my mom. For years, when Lety was struggling, we never did anything fun or normal as a family, like go out to dinner. But now she had shown up and was making her way to us through the crowd, looking pretty and healthy. I unexpectedly felt tears well up in my eyes. When Lety fell into the slipperiness of substance use, we all prayed and prayed for her to get better . . . seemingly to no avail. But here she was, bursting through, like the sun after a storm.

The surrealness of it all continued through dinner when Lety delivered amazing news. "I got hired as a recovery coach!"

She had been in a recovery program for nearly two years and was set to graduate. As part of their job-placement program, she'd been interviewing at rehab centers as a volunteer. One center needed a full-time recovery coach, and she got the job! "So many people applied, but they picked me!" she said, sounding as if she didn't quite believe it herself. "They still have to check my references," she said cautiously, "but they let me know they wanted me!"

We clinked our glasses (iced teas and sparkling waters all around), and I told her, "I'm so proud of you!" I wanted to jump up and tell the whole restaurant, "My sister got a job! My sister got a job!" Instead, I said, "Dad's really proud of you."

I saw a flash of sadness cross her face, though her smile never wavered. Her look reminded me of the "joy-pain" of life the Mexica talked about: to get *here*, my sister had to go through *there*, the joy-pain of this moment where we could *feel* the presence of our father but couldn't put our arms around him or celebrate with him.

But at least we could all feel that burst of joy-pain—however brief—instead of trying to squash it with drink or drugs or any of the other futile coping methods we'd used to get through.

"Wow!" I said incredulously, still taking it all in. "A recovery coach!"

To *recover* means to regain consciousness, to come back, to return. And Lety had come back. To us and, most importantly, to herself. And now, miraculously, she'd get to help others come back to themselves. Though she might never refer to herself as one, she was, truly, a curandera.

The next morning, I walked into the kitchen to grab coffee and noticed the glasses in the cabinet were dusty. I immediately felt the need to clean.

When my mom shuffled in, I told her, "Mom, I'm gonna help you straighten up!" Soon, we started going through cabinets, throwing knickknacks away. Or in truth, I discarded while my mom protested. I picked up a ginormous, used 7-Eleven plastic cup and said, "Really, Mom, you need this?" I didn't wait for a response and tossed it into the overflowing cardboard box of stuff to donate.

As I pulled out a bag of old plastic plug-in air fresheners, Apolonia came in.

"What are you doing, Robyn?" she asked me, annoyed.

"I'm helping Mom clean out the kitchen," I replied breezily.

"I didn't ask you to come into my house and start throwing things away," she said, giving me a dirty look.

I squeezed the trash bag I was holding so hard I could feel my nails digging into my palms. "Apolonia, I am helping Mom clean; maybe you can help us," I said determinedly.

"Oh, so you're the boss of the house now? Ha!" she said, fake laughing. But she left the kitchen.

Fuck! I had only been there for fourteen hours, and we were already slipping into our old ways of fighting.

I let out a big exhale. I needed some caffeine . . . and some air. After going through a drive-through for coffee, we headed over to the big house my dad had built for us. My mom's friend, who lived a block away, told her the house was for sale. It looked exactly like it had thirty years ago. No one was home, so we parked in the circular driveway and walked around the house, peeking in all the windows. I could see a work ladder, as if someone was painting. I looked up to my old bedroom window where I used to climb onto the roof and read my books. I imagined a piece of me still there. Still thirteen years old. Shattered because my dad had just died. I pulled out a dried herb bundle and lit it. I closed my eyes and imagined myself inside my old bedroom. I saw my little white daybed and the pink walls I had chosen myself, feeling so big. And then I saw myself, teenage Robyn, looking out the window intently. Was I looking for something—or waiting for someone to come back?

I gently approached myself and called my own name. And thirteen-year-old me looked up with my own big eyes. "Robyn, I know your heart is hurting," I said to my younger self, who looked so sweet and so sad. "But you are going to be okay; I promise you, mamita, I promise," feeling the truth of that deep in my Ser. I extended my hand out, the same way my father had done in my soul retrieval with Virginia so many months ago. "It's time to come with me now," I said tenderly but firmly. Looking scared but also relieved, teenage Robyn took my hand. In my mind, I held her hand tightly, walked her out of the house, and then hugged her, bringing her back home to me.

Feeling that reconnection, I opened my eyes and stood looking up at my empty window. When I walked back to the front of the house, my mom was standing there, and I lit my bundle again. "Dear spirits of the east, west, north, and south, please release any stuck energy that no longer needs to be here. And please help guide whatever part of ourselves we have left here to come back to us now, to these bodies, our true homes."

I was not surprised to see the house empty. Though we were its very first residents, we never fully occupied this home. We had brought our newly sustoed selves here, moving in six months after my dad died. And frozen it remained. Until now.

Quietly, we got back into our car, and then I asked my mom if it was okay if we went to visit our childhood home. Neither my mom nor I had driven by the small house in over a decade—or longer. Lety had warned us it looked bad—but my mom and I were aghast when we parked in front. The house wasn't just run-down; it was completely abandoned. All the windows were boarded up, and the yard was brown with neglect.

"Wow," exhaled my mom. "This isn't good," she said as we looked at a big trash can that had toppled over in the yard. "This used to be such a sweet house," she said sadly.

I looked at the withering lawn and remembered playing there, chasing my sisters with a water hose. I thought of my mom's rock garden filled with cacti and how every year our dad would make us take a family photo holding our Easter baskets, with our little white house in the background. Now the place looked as if it was about to be demolished.

There were no windows to peer into, so we walked around back. A train track ran behind the yard, and Mom told me that at work, they used to tease her that it was the rumbling of the train that caused her to jump into my dad's arms, resulting in so many kids. I laughed with her, but it was hollow because the appearance of the house was just so *haunting*.

We found a window that used to lead into Lety's room. On a whim, I tried lifting the window, and it opened. I heaved myself in, then put my hand out to my mom, who wisely said, "Just open the front door for me."

I slowly walked through the shell of the house and let my mom in, and I lit that overworked herb bundle. We walked through each room, and my mom described how it used to be. "There was our kitchen," she said like a spooky real estate agent, pointing to an empty area where now wires were hanging from the wall.

We walked through what used to be our little dining room and den. Carpet had been ripped up so that just concrete floors remained, and broken walls revealed beams and insulation. We made our way back up to our one tiny bathroom—the one we all fought for. There was now wood covering up the bathtub where I spent so much time reading, trying to escape the crowd and noise of my house.

Making my way out, I paused to peer into my old bedroom. Toward the right corner where my bed used to be, I saw myself at maybe six or seven years old, holding a stuffed animal and looking scared. This young vision of me was wearing pajamas, and my hair was tousled.

I walked over to where my little bed used to be and picked myself up, as though I was carrying Lucia or Astrid, and gently carried myself out of the house. Once outside in the clean air, I whispered down to myself like a mantra, "You're safe, mamita, you're safe." And as I hugged myself tight, I could *feel* little Robyn dissolve back into me.

I stood there, rooted, for a while; then I made my way to the front, where my mom was standing near the curb, either to get a better look at the monstrosity our house had become or to better distance herself from it.

"This is so terrible!" she said. "What does it mean?"

"I don't know, Mom," I said honestly. "Maybe it represents how bad our home life has become."

I lit the smoke medicine again and was walking forward toward the house to bless it when I saw Lety's name etched into our driveway. She had written it decades ago when they were laying the concrete. My dad was furious at the time, but there it was, enduring.

I walked back to my mom and hugged her. Then, waving the smoke, I said aloud, "We call ourselves back, any pieces of our soul that still remain, we call ourselves back! Any spirits who still linger, you are released! Thank you for protecting the house, but we are all good. It's time for us all to go home!"

"Get it, girl!" the crowd yelled.

The next evening, Lety's recovery program was hosting a formal Christmas party, and she'd bought tickets for us to attend. Lety and I were strutting down a dancing line while a group of women cheered us on. "Yeah!" I yelled when we reached the end; I hugged Lety. She and I hadn't had fun like this, soberly, possibly ever, and I was grateful for it. Over dinner Lety explained that the program director hosted this annual holiday party for her recovery group because she wanted to celebrate the attendees with delicious food, a DJ, loads of presents, and the opportunity to get dressed up. Looking around at the crowd of mostly Black and Latina women—decked out in lots of sequins and bodycon dresses—I understood why the director wanted everyone to feel special, to celebrate their achievements.

A huge percentage of the people who graduated from this particular program stayed sober. They had all endured their own journeys to get here. But here they were. Sober and fabulous. They deserved this party and so much more.

When it was time to leave, Lety wanted me to go back to her house with her to watch movies, but I was anxious to get back to Apolonia. We still hadn't been able to connect, and I felt bad about our interaction that morning. When we got home, Jacob was at work, and Apolonia was gone. Not quite ready to call it a night, my mom and I went to Walmart to get some popcorn so we could watch our own movie.

"The party was so sweet, wasn't it, Mom?" I asked.

"It really was," she said.

"Lety said the organization that runs her program has free mental health and substance use resources. We need that for Apolonia, Mom; she deserves it!"

"Apolonia is fine! You worry too much," chastised my mom.

"You don't worry enough!" I replied.

"Robyn," she said, starting to get angry, "you have no idea about all the things I put up with and handle."

"But you shouldn't have to!"

"You never give me credit for anything!" she yelled.

"Mom, I—" I tried to speak, surprised,

"Give it to me, Robyn! Give me the credit I deserve. Give it to me!"

Underneath the fluorescent lights of the parking lot, my mom looked so tired and old. I just wanted better for her. For all of us.

"I'm sorry, Mom. I know you're doing your best. I . . . I give it to you." I put my arm around her, wishing I could give her much more.

I woke up the next morning feeling tired but ready to do the limpia on the house. After breakfast of bean tamales and coffee, I was tying my red sash under my white shirt when Apolonia walked in.

"Good morning, lady," I said, unsure whether Apolonia was still mad at me.

"It smells good," she said, inhaling the copal I was just beginning to light.

"How are you, mama?" I asked her, trying to find a way in.

She shared some worries she had on her mind about finances and life. And I tried my best to fully listen.

"I can't even imagine how hard this must be for you," I replied, feeling the weight of her pain up close.

"Thanks for listening," she said. "It helps a lot."

"I'm sorry about yesterday, Apolonia," I said simply. "I'm sorry I always act like a bossy big sister. I'm just worried about you."

"I know you are, Robyn," she said, looking straight at me for the first time.

"Do you want a limpia?" I asked.

To my utter shock, she said, "Okay."

I lit the copal and told her to extend her arms out to the sides. I took a deep breath and placed my hand with the smoking copal on the crown of Apolonia's head. "Dear Dad, Mama Natalia, ancestors, and spirits, please help me cleanse Apolonia of anything she doesn't need. Please release what does not belong to her so she can

be happy and at peace . . . in her body, mind, and soul." I then
recited a prayer and circled the copal over her head, mentally trying to cleanse her negative thoughts. I whispered, "You are
cleansed, you are healed, you are loved." I then passed the copal
over her heart, praying that she could keep coming back to her
own self-trust and truth. I kept chanting, "You are cleansed, you
are healed, you are loved."

I inhaled and continued passing the copal along her arms and
imagined that she could hold herself with self-love. "You are
cleansed, you are healed, you are loved." I waved the smoke over
her womb and said, "You are cleansed, you are healed, you are
loved." I moved down her legs and sent her grounding energy.

I rose up and walked around to her back and did it all again, top
to bottom. "You are cleansed, you are healed, you are loved."

When I came around and faced her, her eyes were closed.
"Please, spirits, keep bringing Apolonia back to her heart. She is
love. We are lucky to have her." Apolonia was crying. "You are
beautiful. You are strong. You are loved." I hugged her and whispered, "I love you."

"I love you too, pretty girl," she said.

I didn't know whether the limpia helped ease Apolonia's burdens, but I'd tried. I was done trying to cure the pains of my sister,
but I'd always care for her.

The next morning, my mom and I drove three hours to see Dora.

It was a long drive, but I could not visit Texas and not see my
beloved great-tía. Soon we arrived at a cute brick one-story house,
and Dora's daughter, Naomi, came out to greet us. Then there she
was! La Dora! She used a walker but looked fabulous at ninety-two
years young. She was all gussied up and had a festive red holiday
sweater on.

As we drank coffee, I looked over Dora's gorgeous old photos
while Naomi took my mom to the couch and balanced her chakras.
Naomi was a gifted healer and energy worker too and hilarious to

boot. I instantly adored her and was so glad I was getting to reconnect with family.

"*¿Quieres un buñuelo?*" Dora asked as she brought out the cinnamon treats. As I broke a piece off, Dora told me how on every New Year's Eve, they'd all go out to celebrate, then come home to Mama Natalia, who had stacks of fresh-made buñuelos and Mexican hot chocolate on the table for everyone to enjoy. Like we were enjoying now.

As I looked at the photos on the table, one caught my eye. It was Mama Natalia wearing the ring with four pearls. "Do you still have this ring with pearls?" I asked hopefully, pointing at the picture.

"*¡Ay diosito!* That's not pearls," she said, laughing. "She couldn't afford that. It was four silver balls. She always wore that ring. She said it was for her four favorite things."

"What's that?" I asked excitedly.

"Her children—Jay, Nieves, Lorenzo—and me!"

That's what it meant. It made sense. Her three children and Dora, her first grandchild. The link to the next generation that was connecting us all.

Before we left, I let Naomi balance my chakras. "You're very clear," she commented. She passed over my throat chakra and said, "You don't have any problem speaking your truth, do you, girl?"

I guessed not anymore.

I had come to San Antonio ready to do battle with family and sustos and convince my mom and sisters to do a soul retrieval. And now, heading home, I felt as though I had won some small victories, but somehow the war wasn't over.

Get Rooted Practice #13
Call Yourself Back

There are many ways that we lose ourselves throughout the day.

We expend our energy and essence every day, sharing it at work with colleagues and clients, with friends and loved ones, and even with strangers during our daily interactions. Sometimes, a piece of our energy can stay behind in a place or situation—stuck in a conversation you had with a friend, a conflict you had with a colleague, or a weird interaction you had with a stranger at the store.

To help bring you back to the present, instead of ruminating about your day, try calling your sacred energy essence back home to your body.

Calling yourself back is an integral part of a soul retrieval, a process facilitated by a curandera/o/x that brings a soul piece back home to yourself.

This "call yourself back" practice is like a daily miniature soul retrieval so you can keep your energy intact and mind clear; I first learned about it from my friend and healer Christine Gutierrez.

You can do this practice any time of day, when you find yourself stuck on something that happened hours, days, or weeks ago. But I like doing it in the evening, where it can become part of your bedtime routine.

As you lay your head on your pillow at night, close your eyes and say to yourself, "I call myself back to this moment; I call myself back. I call myself back from where I shared myself today; I call myself back. From all places and all situations, I call myself back. Come back, [your name], come back."

Mentally recount your day—see yourself at work, at the store, with your friends—and then imagine yourself leaving those places and flying back to you and your body. As you see yourself come back, imagine your spirit entering at the crown of your head, and feel yourself expand as your essence reintegrates back into your body, flowing to your heart, filling you up, and rooting you down. Allow the weight and depth of your being to radiate from your heart and outward throughout your body with every inhale and exhale, filling every crevice, and leaving you complete, content, and at peace.

12

Rooting to Rise

"*Venerable Madre, venerable Padre, le pedimos que nos proteja y nos guíe para el trabajo que haremos en los próximos días, en nombre de Quetzalcoatl. Ometeotl!*" said Antonette, our retreat leader.

My hands were raised to the sky, and I was shaking a rattle in ceremony. Understanding my family wouldn't participate in a group soul retrieval the way that I had hoped, I had accepted an invite from Patty to join her in Belize for a retreat. Now here I was, on a ranch in the countryside of Belize, on the banks of the Mopan River, thirty minutes from the Guatemalan border.

Our retreat was led by Antonette, a quiet but powerful wildlife biologist / curandera. She would lead us in our main event, which was a cave healing based on Toltec teachings. Our other maestra was Ms. Chena, the owner of Clarissa Falls, the ranch where we were staying. She grew up on this land and was a gifted herbalist. People came from all over the world for her medicines and concoctions, many of which were grown on her property.

Our third teacher was Alma, Antonette's maestra from Mexico City. After the opening ceremony, Alma gave us a lecture on four Toltec symbols. She explained how the Toltecs flourished before the Aztec empire. As renowned astrologists, artists, and mystics, the Toltec people's wisdom was highly regarded and adopted by the Mexica and Maya.

The first symbol was the spiral, represented by a conch and symbolizing infinity, the cyclical nature of life and the everlasting nature of spirit. Then Alma drew two intertwined snakes. This symbolized duality: joy-pain, yin-yang, masculine-feminine. As a Gemini, my astrological symbol is twins, and I long felt the conflicting pulls of being both an extrovert and introvert.

The next symbol was the number four. Four is powerful—the four directions, the four seasons. The number four represents organization and structure. The last symbol was the number seven. Seven is important because it represents balance, the halfway mark between one and thirteen, the number of transformation and change.

They had laid out bright bowls of fruit and fresh flowers and asked us to play with these materials to create an offering to the altar that utilized one of these symbols. Instinctively, I chose the number four; it felt right. I have three sisters. And Lars, the girls, and I are a family of four. Plus, I was drawn to the idea of organization. Like a four-sided structure, this 260-day journey for me had been a contained falling apart.

To symbolize this architecture and flow, I chose two beautiful radishes and two adorable little red peppers and placed them close together, creating a cozy, bright quadrant. "Four!" I thought. Like the four silver balls on Mama Natalia's ring.

Patty, too, had chosen the number four, and afterward, as we walked to our little cabins wearing headlamps in the darkness, we laughed to find she was staying in room number four.

Patty had arrived earlier than I had that afternoon and had already personalized her casita. She had created an altar on her nightstand, and the room smelled of copal and lavender. She'd laid out her pretty sarongs on top of the simple beds and brought her own portable speaker to play music. When I went to use the rustic bathroom, she had flip-flops laid out and beauty products lined up on her sink. This was Patty: bruja and bougie!

I laid on one of the cozy twin beds and filled Patty in on what had happened in San Antonio over the holidays. "I guess it was naive to think I could *make* my family have a soul retrieval. Like I could wave some magical copal wand, and poof! Everyone would get better."

"Quédate con lo tuyo," said Patty, reminding me of Virginia's wise teaching to stay with my own healing.

I laughed; then, after a pause, I shared with Patty something I had thought about endlessly but couldn't seem to talk about with anyone else. "I wonder how Grandfather's abuse affected my dad. It hurts me to think what he knew or witnessed or even endured."

"Geraldo's abuse has affected all of us, every member of our family," replied Patty, whose older sister Flo had been molested by our grandfather.

The weight of that filled our sweet room.

All along, I had been trying to get my family to do a soul retrieval. In San Antonio, I could see how all of our susto was intertwined, but now that nagging feeling of something simmering below the surface roared up. It all made sense now, my dad's legacy of trauma and ours.

"Patty," I said, feeling things fall into place, "we should do our own family healing."

"Yes!" said Patty instantly. "We can pray and do limpias for them all, for their spirits and ourselves."

Immediately, she pulled out her notepad and began writing down ideas.

There was a beautiful river that ran along the property. "We'll do it in the river," I said.

It made sense.

We would cleanse and reclaim ourselves in *el río*. It felt natural to do family work here beside a river because we grew up on rivers in Texas, and now the currents of our life had brought Patty and me here.

We got so caught up in planning for our family healing, I was surprised to look up and see that it was past midnight. We had to be up for breakfast by eight thirty for a plant walk with Ms. Chena. "I'll text Virginia and ask her for some advice," Patty said as she hugged me good night.

I left the womb of room number four for a short, fragrant walk to my own cabin. As I fumbled for my key, my headlamp illuminated the door, and I saw my own room number and smiled: thirteen. Alma said thirteen was powerful because it represented change. And four equaled structure. Thirteen times four equaled fifty-two. To the Mexica, fifty-two was a sacred number, a complete cycle of life, because their two calendars synced every fifty-two years. So together, Patty and I would come together to start a new cycle of healing for our generation and hopefully the generations to come.

The next morning, after sleeping like the dead, I tiptoed out for breakfast so I didn't wake Mari, my roommate, and took a flowery path along the river to the open-aired cabana that was our eating area. I poured myself some fragrant Belizean coffee and sat next to Olga and Carolina, who were nurses from the Bronx and who had me laughing all through our breakfast—which was the best I have had in my *life*. Even though I was full, I still grabbed a piece of juicy papaya and made room for just one more little homemade corn tortilla filled with refried beans, okra, and a spicy homemade habanero sauce. *Qué rico!*

After breakfast, we piled into two vans and drove eight miles up the road, where Ms. Chena would lead us back on a nature walk along the Mopan River. Four hours later, we arrived back at the ranch, exhausted but filled with all kinds of medicinal knowledge— from boiling the leaves of a local plant to treat *mal de ojo* to treating uterine issues with wild berries.

The highlight was receiving blessings from the base of a ceiba tree, which the Maya considered the tree of life: the roots represent the underworld, the trunk is the present life, and the extending branches point to the thirteen heavens in the sky.

Ms. Chena asked the tree for permission first; then we all got to walk up and embrace it. As I laid my cheek on the cool bark and hugged its solid frame, I felt as though I was leaning into Mama Natalia, our roots entwining us into the ground below.

As we walked back, the rainforest morphed into the open fields of the ranch that looked like a majestic savanna. I had only been here one day, but Clarissa Falls seemed so familiar; I couldn't tell if I was seeing my future or remembering my past.

After a mouthwatering lunch, we gathered in an open-air pavilion for a class on the nine underworlds. Antonette explained the Mexica believed there were nine underworlds that we travel through when we die. The underworlds represent places where our energy can get trapped, like being stuck in addictions, hurtful habits, and ancestral patterns.

Antonette had been studying the Toltec dreaming tradition, a type of wisdom that has been passed down orally, she told us, teacher to student, for hundreds of years. On a whiteboard, Antonette drew an image of a flower with four petals, which represented the four cardinal directions: north, east, south, and west. The center of the flower was our present universe. The buds or flowering stamen reached up and toward the thirteen heavens, while the roots dug down into the nine underworlds. It was believed that we "flower" here on earth by working with our emotions. Antonette explained that hardships like breakups, job losses, or even illness could help us bloom, even though we'd experience that heart-shattering pain that blows us open. She also reminded us that flowers were in motion, swaying in the wind, the same way we should move our bodies, express our emotions, and take action to be of service.

As Antonette took us through each underworld and its meaning, I looked again at the diagram of the flower, the rapturous blossom dancing in the wind, and how it had to push through the dirt to rise.

At dinner, Patty and I sat with Caban, a curandero from Guadalajara. He always wore white and spoke only Spanish. Patty's Spanish was good, and over dinner, we shared why we were there and what our plans were for our family healing. After dinner, we walked back to our cabins under the blanket of shining stars. "Let's stargaze!" I proposed, and we all returned ten minutes later, after retrieving some blankets and binoculars from our rooms. We grabbed three folding chairs from the lecture pavilion and sat on the expansive lawn, looking up at Orion's Belt. Caban had brought his hand drum, called a *tambor*, and he began to play and sing a song about giving thanks to Madre Tierra.

We soon joined in and sang along, not caring if we got the words wrong. "*Yo soy hija de la Tierra, magia de luna y de sol.*" A miraculous thing happened to me when the drum played: I stopped thinking. There was something about the beat and resonance of the drum that brought me straight back into my body. I thought of the drum that Virginia used in the soul retrieval last summer, and my own, which I was playing more and more. In each beat, I felt my dad here.

When Caban was done singing, we asked for advice on how best to conduct our family healing ritual. On our last day we had open time for healings, and Patty and I planned to do it then. Caban smartly asked us what we were healing from, and after pausing, Patty told him about our family trauma of sexual abuse.

He listened quietly throughout, then said in Spanish, "Your grandfather sent you here."

"For the healing?" I asked.

"Yes." He nodded. "But before that, you must forgive him," he said, pointing to the sky. "Your grandfather, he is stuck and in pain. He needs you to release him so he can move on."

"What?" Patty and I both said.

"You want us to forgive our grandfather?" Patty asked incredulously.

"Yes," answered Caban. "Before you do any healing, you must first forgive your grandfather."

"I don't know if we can," said Patty honestly. "My grandfather was a horrible person!"

"You have to," Caban said firmly. He looked at us and asked if we had children.

"I do," I said.

He looked right at me. "He"—he pointed to the sky—"will come back and pass the trauma on to your children," he said gravely. I felt the strong winds grip my heart. Patty still looked in disbelief, but I began to feel some truth to what he was saying. We were trying to cure the rotting leaves, but we had to go to the root. It had always been about the root, hadn't it?

"You are guerreras!" said Caban. He had called us warriors. I don't know how brave I felt, but Caban was saying we had to go back and cut out our family susto so I didn't spread it to my children and *their* children. I had learned so many powerful lessons on this journey: moving the winds, discerning between susto and Ser, learning to honor my own 52 percent. And now the final, and hardest, lesson was asking me to forgive.

The next morning was scheduled for the group cave meditation. It felt like a good cleansing and prep before the family healing ritual Patty and I would do on our last day of the retreat. I got dressed and wrapped the red sashes of protection tightly around my waist and forehead. After breakfast, we drove forty minutes on the Hummingbird Highway and arrived at St. Herman's Blue Hole National Park, which is five hundred acres of tropical rainforest, a blue swimming hole, and St. Herman's Cave, which was used by Maya priests and shamans for sacred ceremonies.

Before we entered the cave, Alma showed us how to be respectful when entering any sacred place. Your left foot signifies strength and power, and your right foot light and radiance. Depending on how you step first, you declare, "I am strength and power" or "I am light and radiance."

We ascended the steps to enter the cave one by one, breathing, "I am strength and power. I am light and radiance." At the cave's entrance, we entered the darkness wearing headlamps. There was a walkway along the right wall, and we held the rope as we descended into the underworld. We made our way down in silence for about fifteen minutes, our headlamps illuminating our path and shining on the stalactites hanging down from the grand ceiling.

Once we got to flat ground, Antonette led us into a small cave off to the side, and we sat in a large circle.

Antonette began our meditation, and speaking in both English and Spanish, she settled us in, telling us to take a few deep breaths:

"*Inhala, exhala* . . . let go of all the heavy energy . . . *connectar a la Pacha Mama, el universo, esta cueva.* We are going to release all the things that keep us trapped in the invisible prison of our minds."

She told us to visualize a feathered jaguar and to put that image in our navel. She explained jaguars can see in the dark. "She's gonna help take you to the underworlds and travel with you to help you see what you cannot see." She had us breathe nine times with the vision of the jaguar to go into a deeper trance. Then we were ready to go.

As we rode into these underworlds to take back our energy, Antonette instructed us to visualize a bonfire. There we were to throw away what was no longer needed. My mind flew to all the things I had retrieved these past months and the things I had let go of. I thought of Virginia telling me way back that self-doubt was colonized thinking. I walked to the fire, in the cave of my imagination, and I saw Mama Natalia standing there. I finally felt ready to throw in the fear that had held me back from walking this path of the medicina. The fear of my own power.

"Let it burn!" said Antonette, and I did.

I got back on my brilliantly colored jaguar, and we rode deeper into an underworld that represents the repetitive patterns that keep us stuck. I thought of how I often ran late, then how I over-booked myself. I was trying to choose a habit to break when a voice in my mind yelled, "You're doing this wrong!" I realized this idea of "you're doing this wrong" had followed me around my whole life.

But after so many months of releasing old stories and ways of being, in that darkness I could finally see that maybe it wasn't me who was wrong. Maybe the rules, this game, was wrong. This game of conforming and denying, of falling in line with whatever the dominant power structure claimed was true. I have always had a deep sense that I was doing it all wrong, but it was not because I was unworthy or messed up or less than. It was because I had the deep knowing that I wasn't supposed to be doing or living like this. I was *right*. Naming these wrongs was right. Saying "none of this makes sense" was right. I felt dizzy for a second as I felt a weight come back into my body.

I walked to the bonfire in my mind and threw "you're doing this wrong" in with both hands.

When I came back to Antonette's voice, she asked us to throw away family patterns that kept knocking us down. I thought of my sisters' and my struggle with substance use and the idea that family loyalty comes first and that things stay inside the house, even dark secrets. I gladly burned it all.

I flew my rainbow jaguar deeper into an underworld where we burned through heavy emotions, like anger or jealousy, that ate our hearts and made us sick. I remembered screaming all that bilis into the dirt months ago. I thought of the anger that my father felt, that my family felt. I threw it all into the fire.

Soon, we were in the underworld where we let go of our attachment to the material world and trusted our inner vision. Reconnecting to my Ser was one of the greatest lifelines. I let go of looking outside myself for approval. I released it all into the fire.

We finished in the final underworld: the place of peace. We'd made it.

As we all gradually came to, Caban began playing the drum, and I grabbed a rattle. Someone started dancing, sweeping away the energy and closing the circle. We quietly got up and gathered ourselves. Patty handed me a shawl, and I put it on in silence. Wearing our headlamps, we wordlessly made our way out of the cave.

In the bright sunlight, we were warmed back into our bodies and walked over to the blue swimming hole to eat and cleanse. We slowly began talking, sharing experiences, and someone commented on my shawl. Only then did I see it had the pattern of a hummingbird.

We had come to the last day of our retreat, and it was time for the family healing ritual Patty and I had devised. We set up an altar by the river with the bright purple, pink, and yellow flowers we had found on the property at Clarissa Falls. I was wearing a white dress with a red sash and my red *banda* around my third eye. Caban gave us each a piece of copal to tape into our belly buttons for protection. Patty and I took turns giving each other a limpia, passing our lit sahumerios over each other.

Then Patty began by calling on the directions of the west and the north to guide us. Because we had already opened the group circle by praying to the directions on our first day here, we were instructed by Alma to begin our private ceremony by invoking just two directions: to the west, the direction of letting go; and to the north, the direction of our ancestors. While Patty was speaking, Caban hit his drum, and I shook my rattle.

Then we began our ritual by calling in our grandfather. Caban had warned that I must forgive this man who had done so much harm. As much as I respected Caban, what I had really learned throughout this journey was that the "must" I had to listen to was that of my own Ser. I could never let an outside authority, even a well-intentioned one, override the truth of my own heart. And that truth said that I was not fully ready to forgive my grandfather. I must honor that. Trusting myself and speaking my truth—*that* is how I would break the cycles for my kids.

I knew I couldn't forgive my grandfather on behalf of my cousin Flo or others he had hurt, though Flo told me that she *had* forgiven him. I also knew I couldn't even forgive him on behalf of my father. That was their healing; I had to stay with mine. The word *mercy* means "price paid" in Latin. We had all paid the price for our grandfather's actions. I couldn't 100 percent forgive my grandfather, this man I never met whose harm infected the bloodstream of our family. But in my heart, I felt a jagged pain that was ready to be released. I was willing to try, to show him and us all mercy, so we could move on. So I did.

Patty and I both walked into the river, and it was slipperier than we thought. The sun was setting fast now, and darkness was settling in. We walked toward the middle, and holding on to a rock, we cleansed ourselves.

Then we spoke aloud to the river and the trees our truth at that moment: that we were willing to try to show mercy to our grandfather for his actions so we could cut the ties of susto and move on. We decided we would take each of his children and one by one, spiritually cleanse, release, and bless them and all of their descendants down to the grandkids and those still to come. Patty started while I passed the smoking sahumerio filled with copal over her front and back, and then she immersed herself in the river.

Next, I asked Oscar, my dad's brother who was shot and killed when he was just a teenager, to be our angel and guide and to free his spirit—wherever he was—from trauma. Patty passed the sahumerio over me; then I dunked myself in the river.

Next was my dad. "Dear ancestors, spirits, and guides," I said, "please release my dad from the pain of his childhood. I forgive him for his hurtful actions and words and for any trauma and anger he passed on to us."

Then I prayed for my sisters, mom, and nephews. I prayed for them to be healed and freed from the susto that had plagued our family. Then I prayed for myself and my family. "Please release my susto and allow me to move forward, cleansed and whole. And for my children, Lucia and Astrid, to walk free, light, joyful, unsustoed, and blessed through their lives and the lives of their children and so on." Then I dove under the water, releasing it all to the river. We closed the ceremony with a poem I'd written.

In the sacred waters we are born, their medicina is where we swim
Here we were called to show mercy to the wounded souls we call kin
In the river sustos fall away; only love and Ser can stay
That has always been our way
Past, present, and future entwine,
Cleansed and healed until the end of time.

The next day we closed the circle. The retreat was over, but our journey, in many ways, had just begun. There was an airport-closing snowstorm back in New York, so Patty and I decided to travel to the closest beach to enjoy two more days until they could rebook us.

We arrived smack into the tiny town of Hopkins and ran straight to the beach. Looking out onto the clear blue ocean, I felt like I had never seen anything so beautiful in my life.

Patty and I each rented matching yellow bungalows on stilts, and after resting for a bit, I walked out and sat down on the sand. There was not one person on the beach. Then, gazing to the left, I was struck by something familiar. *This is it!* This was the place I had been meditating about for years. It looked so familiar I almost expected my dad to sit down next to me. And in my mind, he did. Though I could not have imagined any of this 240 days ago, I was not at all surprised to be here now. I didn't know where I was going when I started this journey, but somehow I had arrived.

I walked into the welcoming water, and, flipping onto my back, with the depths below and the sky above, I surrendered into a sea of forgiveness . . . but this time for myself. I forgave myself for all the many mistakes I made, some when I didn't know any better, but some when I did and acted against myself anyway. I forgave myself for waging war against my own being, my own body, and my own dreams for so long. I forgave myself for losing my way—sometimes purposefully—again and again. I forgave myself for ignoring my Ser; for hiding my own light. I forgave myself for being fractured and also for wanting to be whole. I forgave myself for slipping and for having the audacity to get back up.

I forgave myself for surviving and thriving when others had not. I forgave myself for resisting this journey for so long. I forgave myself for not getting here sooner.

I floated like this effortlessly and endlessly, yet anchored in my Ser, rooting me into the eternal waters of my home.

Get Rooted Practice #14
A Gentle Self-Forgiveness Ritual

To forgive those who have hurt us is hard and healing and a personal journey of if, when, and how. But forgiveness, as we understand it, is layered and takes time. Rather than forcing or pushing yourself to forgive when you are not ready, you can begin to open the door by forgiving yourself first.

This practice is adapted from a self-forgiveness ritual given to me by my maestra Virginia. And because all of our healing looks different, feel free to adapt or adjust as it makes sense for you.

Go to a body of water. It can be a stream, river, pond, lake, or ocean—whatever is convenient and calls to you. Think of something you need to forgive yourself for. I suggest by starting with something that isn't so heavy, such as an instance when you let yourself down or acted against your own best interest. I am purposefully suggesting you start small so that you can heal those hurts and gather your strength. I understand the urge toward big, fast, and dramatic healing, but it's safer and more soothing for our soul and well-being to have slow and real change.

Think of the thing you need to forgive yourself for. Feel whatever feelings come up: remorse, embarrassment, sadness. Then grab a nearby rock, leaf, or shell, and say aloud, "I forgive myself." Repeat "I forgive myself" eight more times, feeling your loving touch infuse this item in your hand. If the word "forgive" is not resonating with you, you can try something like "love" or "accept." Then release it into the water, watching it go. This is a practice that reminds us to be gentle with ourselves.

You can come back to this simple but powerful ritual as you need. And remember, just the *willingness* to forgive yourself, to show yourself mercy, even just a handful, opens the door for healing and love to shine through.

PART FIVE

The Fifth Direction: Connecting It All

13

Writing a New Flower Song

What is a healing?

That was the question I had been pondering since I returned from Belize.

Coming back from the retreat, I felt calmed and cleansed—and changed. Like the Robyn who went to Belize wasn't the same one who came back. Instead of feeling euphoric or wise, I immediately got sick: flush with fever, achiness, and a sore throat—all coupled with a moon cycle so intense I found myself running to the bathroom with blood dripping down my legs.

"You are releasing," said Virginia after I reached out, reeling from the aftershocks of the healing. "This is normal after a deep cleansing," my maestra assured me, though I was no longer sure what *normal* was. With only weeks now until the end of this 260-day journey, I felt like a wet butterfly emerging from my cocoon. Broken out of the chrysalis, but not ready to fly just yet. When I conceived this journey, I hadn't thought about—or prepared for—the *post*-healing, where I would know how to make my way in the world. And my world really meant Lars and my girls. I had come to the fifth and final direction. The culmination and integration of everything I had learned in the east, north, west, and south. The last direction represents community and connection. It reminds us that we are all small pieces of a greater whole and that our healing affects those before and after us.

The very last task of the journey was to pass on the medicine to my children. But although I may have dramatically imagined a scene where I sat with them on a cliff, blowing copal and showing them the way like a wise elder, I could see now that "passing on the medicine" wasn't simply teaching Lucia and Astrid about Curanderismo. It was about choosing which medicine, traditions, and ways of being were ours, what was true to *us,* and learning to practice those in our lives. It was not about standing on mountains or sitting in caves; it was about using what I had learned climbing mountains—and exploring that cave—to get rooted into the here and now so I could steadily lead (and also follow) my children wherever they needed to go.

In Belize—and throughout this journey—I had burned family trauma and patterns; I knew the kind of parent I didn't want to be. But feeling raw and reborn, I was honestly trying to learn and remember what kind of parent and person I *did* want to be. And the challenge of parenting post-healing came to a head in a telling moment.

In addition to feeling sick after I returned from Belize, I was suffering from a lack of sleep because Astrid's nighttime routine had been off. She had always been a tough sleeper, but since I got back from the trip, she had woken up every night, yelling for us. It was like having a newborn in the house again, and I was starting to lose it. One exhausted morning, I woke late and came downstairs as Lars was putting Lucia's and Astrid's coats on to leave for school.

Though Lars had fed and clothed the girls and brushed their teeth so I could sleep in, all I could focus on was their messy hair. I furiously grabbed the brush out of a drawer, and the girls immediately started running away from me—which only infuriated me more. I yanked the brush through Astrid's thin, short baby hair, and she let out a howl. Then I grabbed Lucia, sat her down on the bench we had in our mudroom, and roughly pulled off the neck warmer she was wearing. It had a toggle that hit her on the head, and she yelped in protest. I then forcefully brushed her long, stringy, tangled hair while she screamed bloody murder. Lars came in to see what was happening just as I stopped myself.

I had just replayed a scene from my childhood, and, holding the brush in the air, I felt a wave of scary recognition. I instinctively hugged and consoled Lucia and Astrid. After watching my family head out for school, I went upstairs, sat in front of my altar, and cried.

My parents were hitters and yellers. And even though I loved them fiercely, I didn't want to be them. I didn't want to parent like this.

"A healer is *always* healing," Virginia gently reminded me when I told her about my parenting struggles. I had forgiven my ancestors, as much as I could at the moment, but now what would I do with the future? How would I parent my own children? If I truly wanted to break the patterns, I had to do something different. After much research, I enrolled in a course called Decolonized Nonviolent Parenting.

And because I tend to overthink, I started art therapy so I could quiet my mind as I dropped into my body to paint. In my first session with the art therapist, she asked me to draw how I was feeling. I immediately started drawing blue waves of water. I drew them again and again. I was lost in the water when I noticed her looking at me. Instantly, I felt self-conscious, like these squiggly lines weren't what she wanted. So then I immediately added a sailboat with a family on it under a shining sun with birds flying around. We discussed the idyllic image: a family navigating their way through a sunny existence together.

But soon we made our way back to the water. The waves I kept drawing again and again. I had been churned up since that morning with Lucia and Astrid, and I was trying to work it out here. I told this to the therapist, and we went back and looked at the sunny drawing of the family.

Then she asked, "How is this different from that morning with the girls?"

"This is the opposite! That morning felt raging and out of control."

"So is this your family ideal?" she asked me. "Smooth sailing?"

"Yes," I said, laughing.

"The sea can change," she reminded me. "Sometimes it's calm, but sometimes it is stormy, right?"

"And it can be slippery and slick," I thought.

"What else do you see?" she asked me.

"Well," I thought out loud, looking at the image, "it is sunny and happy, but things can get cloudy; that's true." She stayed quiet and looked at me, waiting for me to continue. "But we have the safety of our boat, and we have each other."

"Yes, you have *each other*. You and Lars and the girls are a team. You are the parent, and, yes, it is your responsibility to steer this ship; the girls need your guidance. But don't be afraid of the storms. Parenting is not always smooth sailing," she said.

I must have looked unsure because she added, "And you are not your mom, and you're not your dad. You know how to steer your boat. And let Lars and the girls help you. They might even steer you to places you haven't even imagined."

So much of parenting is really reparenting ourselves. I learned that in my Decolonized Nonviolent Parenting class, where we were encouraged to create new family values, which would be guiding principles on which to parent.

Heeding the advice to let the girls help us navigate our way, at dinner, I asked everyone to help me. "What's important to us as a family?" I asked.

Lucia replied, "That we go to Sweden every summer!" I looked at Lars. "What value is that? Family?"

"Roots," he replied.

Staying in touch with our roots—I liked that. "Roots and cultural heritage," I noted mentally.

Next, I turned to Astrid. "Astrid, what's important to you as a family?"

"Ketchup!" she said, dipping a fish stick in her ketchup. We all laughed.

"Okay, I'll interpret that as the importance of good food and eating together as a family." I looked at Lars. "Babe, you're up."

He didn't miss a beat. "Less screen time. No phones at the table," he said, looking at me. "Bike riding, playing cards, just being together and not distracted."

"Got it, loud and clear," I said, looking around the table at my adorable family. "Let's see. How about we take that as being present and putting family first?"

It was my turn. What was really important to me as a family? "Let's be kind to each other," I said. "And no yelling."

They all looked at me because I was the resident yeller.

"Maybe y'all can help me by listening when I tell you to brush your hair?" I said, looking at the girls.

"Maybe you can listen, Mommy, when I tell you I don't like brushing my hair," said Lucia. "It hurts."

Whaaaat? I looked at Lars, who smiled back at me.

"Okay, Lucia," I said with an honest laugh. "You are right."

"Mama, you never brush your hair!" Astrid added in her baby voice, clearly feeling emboldened.

It was true; I never brushed my hair.

"Okay, okay!" I felt the pile on. "How about this? Y'all can brush your own hair," I said. "And I'll help you if you need." I think Lars and the girls were on Team No Brushing Ever, but everyone nodded, and it felt like this was a good compromise.

Looking over our list of family values later, I felt I'd had some of these things in my childhood, while others I'd only wished for. But the real gift of this past year was that I knew I could do things differently. I was creating my own home, with our own values.

Pulling from the best of what I grew up with—and having the courage to leave the rest behind.

"Sitting in chair pose, bring your hands to your heart. Inhale, bringing your left elbow outside of your right knee."

I had come to a chakra-balancing yoga class, and as I twisted and extended my torso, I thought back to when Virginia had told me in our very first session together that my father's unchecked anger and unreleased emotions may have led to his illness. I thought of this now as I reached and stretched and breathed, trying to balance the emotions about my family—the past and the future. Wrung out, I was lying on my yoga mat in corpse pose when the yoga teacher recited a quote from the poet Mark Nepo: "To be broken is no reason to see all things as broken."

To be broken is no reason to see all things as broken. As I exhaled, I thought about my own brokenness and healing. Even though I had retrieved so many pieces, I knew I might never be done, and that was okay. Instead of seeing the susto in everyone around me, I now clearly saw the bravery and goodness that somehow kept them going. Then I thought of my dad, and something so major dawned on me that I started to cry.

My dad had broken his cycle. My grandfather had hurt his family. My father, though profoundly hurt, protected us. Maybe sometimes too fiercely, but he was reaching for better. My father was offered the worst role model, and he turned away from him—and toward us. He moved the winds. He created boundaries that he didn't grow up with, and he kept them. Even though he was triggered, hurt, and damaged, he did better. He lived it so we wouldn't have to. Maybe that was the work of my dad's lifetime, to break that horrific cycle.

We all want to break generational cycles. For most of us, it is the work of our lifetimes. But the truth is that we still repeat the patterns. We are all the repeaters *and* the breakers. But that's how we find the fault lines. That is the whisper of the susto: it's the soul calling to be found. So we move toward soul, and we fight. We fight for ourselves and our children, and we struggle to do things differently, to change the course, to move the line. To make new maps and create new legacies.

In his children, my father saw our unbrokenness, and hopefully we reflected back his own. And on that mat, with wet tears streaming down my face, I found my own unbroken truth: healing is the greatest act of love and rebellion that you can do. That was the medicine I'd pass on to my children.

With Valentine's Day getting closer, I was trying to figure out how to wind down the project. I called Virginia and asked her whether I should do a closing ceremony.

"Closure is very important," said Virginia, "but is it time to close the circle, comadre?"

"I don't know," I admitted.

"We live in a society that wants to meet the deadline," said Virginia. "Have things done in thirty days!"

Or 260 in my case.

"But this is curandera's time. Don't put a time limit on your healing," warned Virginia. "Go back to your emotions, again and again; you are the healer now."

That is how I would heal—again and again—on curandera's time.

A few days later, my mom called. I hadn't spoken with her since I got back from Belize.

"Hey, Mama," I said.

"What are you doing?" she asked.

"I'm cooking for the kiddos," I replied as I stirred some rice on the stove.

"How was your trip?" she asked.

"It was amazing," I replied honestly.

"What did you do?"

"Well, it was a healing retreat, so Patty and I did some ceremonies, and we prayed for the family."

"Our family?" she asked.

"*All* of our family. Patty and I prayed for healing around the sexual abuse from Geraldo and everyone who was affected. And I prayed for all of us. I prayed for Apolonia. For her peace and for her healing."

"Well, maybe what you did worked because Apolonia has been really good," she said.

"What do you mean?" I asked.

"Since your visit, she's signed up for Medicaid. And she has a job interview, and she's getting ready for it."

"Wow!" I said. "Tell her I said I love her."

After we hung up, I went upstairs and lit a candle. Way back at the beginning of this journey, I had learned my very first lesson of curanderismo by understanding that if we approached the messy people and places in our lives with the humble willingness to support instead of the obsessive need to fix, then the caring became the cure. I honestly didn't know whether I had helped my sisters heal in any way, but I was so happy to hear that Apolonia was doing better. I thought of Lety employed as a recovery coach and of Paloma having fun and being happy in her heart and home.

The biggest lesson I had learned was that I didn't have control over other people's lives, as painful as that was. The earth was slippery slick, and people would fall. The only thing I could do was to get rooted in my Ser so I could keep walking this path and provide stability for my own children, my family, and those who needed it.

The night before Valentine's Day, Lucia, Astrid, and I were sitting at our dining room table, writing out cards to all their classmates. Astrid saw her name on the class list the teacher sent home and started to make a card for herself—when I stopped her. "Astrid, we give cards to *others*," I said instinctively.

Lucia followed my lead and said, "Yeah, Astrid, only if we have extras, we can make our own."

Watching Lucia model me, I realized how wrong I was. In all her innocence and unbrokenness, Astrid was right: we should give ourselves our own valentines! I thought back to my own lessons of worthiness. What I told Astrid was incorrect, but I could fix it.

"Hey, girls, I made a mistake! We definitely should write Valentine's Day cards to ourselves!"

Astrid couldn't really spell yet, so I helped her write her name on her card, an adorable snow cone that said, "You're so chill!"

Lucia's tiny turtle-themed card couldn't hold all her self-love and importance, so I gave her a big card. On it, in her childlike scrawl, she wrote, "I love myself, because I can go anywhere and be anything I want and love to do a lot, like my hobby is writing, and my thing to do is drawing. I love to bike!" She drew four little red hearts and signed her card, "From Lucia to Myself."

I borrowed one of Lucia's little turtle cards and was writing myself my own valentine when Astrid said, "Hey, those are for kids!"

"I am a kid!" I protested as I wrote out R-o-b-y-n on top of the tiny turtle.

Later that night, after the girls had gone to bed, I was so nervous I couldn't sleep. It was exactly the way I felt the night before I started this journey, 259 days ago. I opened a journal and started writing:

Day 259

Looking back at the past eight and a half months, I wonder if I've changed. I read once that a giant boat couldn't feel itself change course because it was too big. Its movements of turning in the water were so slow and gradual, it was hard to feel until you found yourself looking in a completely new direction.

I couldn't see my own changes—it was too soon—but I really was looking down a new path. On my way here:

I had learned about Mama Natalia, my ancestry, and the magic of Curanderismo.

I had become closer to my cousins and aunts, especially Dora, Patty, and Flo.

I had been told I was rooted.

I had clearer boundaries with everyone, including my own family.

I had dropped old stories.

I had made new friends.

I could cook a killer pozole.

I knew how to negotiate a higher wage and believed that I was worth negotiating for.

I had fallen in love with my husband even more.

I had returned to my childhood home, retrieved missing parts of my soul, and healed my gran susto.

I had shown mercy to my ancestors.

I had forgiven my parents.

I had forgiven myself.

I was becoming a more present parent.

I finally stopped drinking.

I understood a healer was always healing.

The next morning, on Valentine's Day, the kids and Lars woke me up. They had a surprise. Lars had made me a wooden altar. He had been down in the basement secretly working on something for weeks, and this was it! He had carved it from the wood of our Douglas fir outside, whittled from the towering tree in our yard I had used to orient myself 260 days ago.

Underneath the altar, he had etched, "To my wife, happy Valentine's Day." Even though Lars didn't always understand what I was doing with this project, he had been as steady and supportive as this wooden table he had made for me. And I knew he had changed too.

This was love.

After I dropped the girls off at school, I ordered my sisters and mom flowers. My father loved Valentine's Day and always used to come home after work with a bouquet of flowers and boxes of chocolates. I was reclaiming the tradition.

Then I called my mom.

My father's last name is Moreno, which means "dark," while my mother's last name is Vela, which means "candle." Throughout this journey, and for most of my life, it was my dad who I was searching for, but it was my mom who had been holding the light. In all my times of darkness, lost in my sustos and pain over my dad, my mom had always been there. Her glow sometimes flickered with her own struggles, but she was my constant presence, the ceaseless star illuminating my slippery slick path. When she answered, I told my mom that I loved her, and she said she loved me too, something I had never, ever doubted.

That afternoon, I went to Lucia's school. I had volunteered to bring a fruit platter for her Valentine's Day party. It was also a publishing party because her class had been working on a book. She had been telling me for weeks now, but like the altar Lars had made me, it was a secret. So when I sat down in her tiny chair, I was blown away. She had written a book about her family. The first page was a dedication page, and she dedicated her book to me, Lars, and Astrid "because I love them so much and there [sic] special to me." The second page was a drawing of us four in our house. I was taller than Lars, which was not at all true in real life, but I loved that I appeared large to her. I thought months back to when a curandero told me that "susto makes you shrink." Maybe being embodied and rooted made me look bigger.

The next page was a photo from Christmas. The girls were wearing traditional Swedish St. Lucia outfits. Lars must have helped Lucia with this. And then the next page brought me to tears.

It was her family tree. She had drawn her face in the middle of the tree, and I was directly on top. On one side was Lars and on the other was Astrid. Right next to her, shooting out on branches, were my mom and dad. My dad had round eyes and gray hair and a lopsided smile. That must be how she imagined him. I was so happy that she imagined him! Below my parents were Lars's parents: Lars's mom, Greta, and Lars's deceased dad, Leif. At the base of the tree was a red heart with her initials. The pages after that were drawings of visits to Sweden and Texas. She had even colored a picture of her cousins. On the last page, we were instructed to write her a note. I wrote:

> *Lucia,*
>
> *Mama and Papa love you so much. We dreamed of you long before you were born. You are kind and funny and brave and so artistically talented. You are a wonderful big sister and an amazing daughter. You are so loved and can do anything you want! We love you as you are and will always have your back. Love Mama, Papa, and Astrid.*

My girls knew who they were. They knew their family; they knew they were loved. More than anything, they were rooted.

That night we went out to eat at Lupe's. The girls brought Lupe flowers, and we basked in the warmth of her kitchen. Afterward, we went home and built an altar together. On it, Astrid placed a homemade heart she'd made, and Lucia drew me a symbol that looks like two banners intertwined with a red dot in the middle. She told me, "It's the Estonian symbol of the dead. My art teacher taught me how to make it. It helps guide dead people home." I honestly had no idea how this would even come up in an art class. But I looked at the little bruja and smiled.

We placed fruit and photos on the altar, then Lars lit a fire, and we broke out the playing cards. We were all happily engrossed in the game, laughing and screaming, when I felt a presence. I looked up, and for a moment, I saw my dad there, playing with us. My dad had died around seven o'clock—and that was the time the clock read now. He was here. I could feel his weight in my bones.

Sitting by the fire, I knew that the river of my soul had thawed. It had been frozen for an achingly long time, but now it was flowing. Maybe that's what healing was: an unfreezing, a remembering, an apology, a forgiveness, the rooting shift that occurs when you can finally see everything you are and have instead of everything you mistakenly thought you were missing—or never knew you had. And in that watery completion lives our unbreakable Ser, flowing from them to him to me to her, caressing and releasing us all.

Get Rooted Practice #15
Write a New Flower Song

The Mexica called poems "flower songs" and held both poets and poetry as sacred. Story is powerful medicina. For most of our lives, someone else has written our narratives. Rewriting our story is our soul retrieval.

Rooted where you are now, what is the new, true story you can write?

Sit down and write a letter to your future descendants. Descendants can be your children, nieces and nephews, godchildren, students, mentees, young friends, and future generations. Explain to them why it was so important for you to go on this journey, what you have learned, and what you hope for them to learn.

You are holding the pen. You are the poet; your life is the poem. Will you leave them a legacy of susto or soul? It is up to you.

This is what we have been working toward. This is the blessed truth: You are your own healer. You are the curandera.

Notes

Chapter 1: Finding Your Way

1. Elena Avila, *Woman Who Glows in the Dark* (New York: Penguin, 1997).
2. Miguel León Portilla, *Aztec Thought and Culture* (Norman: University of Oklahoma Press, 1963), 21.

Chapter 2: Moving the Winds

1. Erika Buenaflor, *Sacred Energies of the Sun and Moon* (Rochester, VT: Bear, 2020).
2. "Species-at-Risk List," *United Plant Savers Medicinal Plant Conservation*, https://unitedplantsavers.org/species-at-risk-list/.
3. Joie Davidow, *Infusions of Healing: A Treasury of Mexican-American Herbal Remedies* (New York: Simon & Schuster, 1999).
4. Dr. James Maffie, *Aztec Philosophy* (Boulder: University Press of Colorado, 2014).
5. Avila, *Woman Who Glows in the Dark*.
6. Avila, *Woman Who Glows in the Dark*.
7. Atava Garcia Swiecicki, *The Curanderx Toolkit* (Berkeley: Heyday, 2022); Jesús C. Villa, "African Healing in Curanderismo" (master's thesis, Arizona State University, 2016), 103, https://keep.lib.asu.edu/items/154360.

Chapter 3: Is It Susto or Ser?

1. D. Alegria, E. Guerra, C. Martinez, and G. G. Meyer, "El Hospital Invisible: A Study of Curanderismo," *Archives of General Psychiatry* 34, no. 11 (1977): 1354–1357.

Chapter 4: Setting Your Table

1. A sahumerio is also called a *popoxcomtl* in Nahautl and can also be called a copalera.
2. Miguel Léon-Portilla, *Fifteen Poets of the Aztec World* (Norman: University of Oklahoma Press, 1992).

Chapter 5: Becoming Remothered

1. "Epatl," *Nahuatl Dictionary*, Wired Humanities Projects, https://nahuatl.wired-humanities.org/content/epatl.

2. Luz Calvo and Catriona Rueda Esquibel, *Decolonize Your Diet: Plant-Based Mexican-American Recipes for Health and Healing* (Vancouver: Arsenal Pulp, 2015).

Chapter 6: The Smoking Mirror

1. Martin H. Teicher and Gordana D. Vitaliano, "Witnessing Violence Towards Siblings: An Understudied but Potent Form of Early Adversity," *PLOSOne* 6, no. 12 (December 21. 2011): e28852, https://www.ncbi.nlm .nih.gov/pmc/articles/PMC3244412/.
2. Atava Garcia Swiecicki, *The Curanderx Toolkit* (Berkeley: Heyday, 2022).

Chapter 7: Building Your Medicine Bag

1. Davidow, *Infusions of Healing*.
2. Sergio Magaña, *Caves of Power: Ancient Energy Techniques for Healing, Rejuvenation and Manifestation* (Carlsbad, CA: Hay House, 2016), 14.

Chapter 8: Reclaiming Your Worth

1. Kate Slater, "The 'Glass Cliff': How Women and People of Color Are Set Up to Fail in the Workplace," Today, August 28, 2020, https://www.today .com/tmrw/glass-cliff-why-women-people-color-are-often-set-fail-t18 9060.

Chapter 9: Coming Back to Your Body

1. Avila, *Woman Who Glows in the Dark*.

Chapter 10: Following the Hummingbird

1. Christopher Soto, "Nepantla and Gloria Anzaldúa's Queer of Color Legacy," *The Millions*, January 17, 2019, https://themillions.com/2019/01/nepantla -and-gloria-anzalduas-queer-of-color-legacy.html.
2. Erika Buenaflor, *Curanderismo Soul Retrieval* (Rochester, VT: Bear, 2019).

Acknowledgments

I firmly believe healing is in the collective, and there are countless souls who supported my journey to healing and helped with the writing of this book. But I want to thank a few. To my fearless agent, Johanna Castillo, who shepherds so many Latinx writers and who got me from the start. Thanks for guiding me, believing in this book since the beginning, and standing by me to the end. *¡Te amo!*

To my brave, brilliant editor and comadre, Renee Sedliar. You were meant to edit this book. Thanks for having the vision to see what this book could become. You are a champion and a seer. To the entire team at Hachette Go: Mary Ann Naples, Michelle Aielli, Julianne Lewis, Michael Barrs, Zachary Polendo, Alison Dalafave, Amanda Kain, and Amber Morris—thanks for helping me take this baby to the world.

To my dear friend and editor, Meghann Foye. You more than anyone saw this book from idea to reality. Your endless belief in me—and this project—carried me through many tough times. I love you.

To Irasema Rivera, my prairie dog, this book was a long time coming, and your stellar design direction and friendship never wavered. *¡Mil gracias!*

Huge love to my book doulas: Erasmo Guerra, Suzan Colón, Jessica Rodriguez, Miles Doyle, Amy Shearn, Christie Jimenez, Marisol Ybarra, Sara Alvarez Kleinsmith, Agnes Im, Joanne Hinkel,

Suzanne Rust, Nicola Wheir, María José Peñaherrera, Mariella Salazar, Asha Frost, and Jesús Cuauhtémoc Villa. And mil gracias to my comadre Atava Garcia Swiecicki for your keen curanderx eye. And thanks to Claudia Serrato, Indigenous culinary anthropologist, for your deep knowledge and recipe testing.

To all of my students and beautiful clients who have given me the honor of being your maestra and guide. Thanks for trusting me! You are my teachers.

To mis comadres—Audrey and Sunday Ponzio, Carmen Wong, Carmen Hernandez, Anne Fritz, Lisa Martin Louro, Rebeca Ramirez, Sammy Smith Coleman, Molly Fyfe, Shirley Velasquez, Ivette Manners, Michelle Herrera Mulligan, Sokhna Heathyre Mabin, Connie Hough, and Ashley Jimenez—thanks for always having my back.

To my sober sisters, I am here because of you.

Big love to Masha Schmidt, Taylor Jackson, Maddie Hamer, Nora Matz, and the rest of our Day Dream Collaborative Clinic. Let's keep dreaming.

Thanks to my local hiking crew and all the friends who supported me in countless ways year after year as I worked on my book. It's done—we can finally hang out! Thanks especially to my dear friend Kenny Davis. I finally hit send.

To my dear friends at the Omega Institute, thanks for always inspiring my growth: Sarah Urech, Carla Goldstein, and Elizabeth Lesser.

To my teachers: Mi maestra preciosa, Virginia, I hit the jackpot when I met you. Your *sabiduría* has changed my life and undoubtedly those of countless others. You are a gift we are lucky to have. To Rita Navarette, Antonette Gutierrez, Alma and Xolot, Patricia Chicueyi Coatl, Azucena Galvez, Bob Vetter, Laurencio Lopez Nuñez, Elin Gwyn, Sergio Magaña, Erika Buenaflor, "Cheo" Torres, Clarissa Pinkola Estés, and countless others for your wisdom teachings and carrying on the medicina. To maestra Elena Avila, I feel like I know you. Thank you for writing down your wisdom that served as a guide to finding my way home.

To Berenice Dimas of Hood Herbalism, Leslie Priscilla Arreola Hillenbrand of Latinx Parenting, Dr. Manuel X. Zamarripa and Tlazoltiani Jessica Zamarripa of the Institute of Chicana/o/x Psychology, Rosalia Rivera of About Consent, and Drena Fagen of New York Creative Arts Therapists, thank you for your work and wisdom. I am better for you.

Thank you to Mexica philosophy professors Sebastian Purcell, James Maffie, Camilla Townsend, and Miguel Léon-Portilla, all of whose diligent work I am indebted to.

To my great-aunt Dora, RIP. I am endlessly grateful for our platicas. Thanks for passing on the wisdom.

To mi Mama Natalia, I wish I had spent more time with you. I carry the medicina in your honor.

To my ancestors, transitioned and unknown, keep flowing to me. You live in my heart. To my aunts and cousins, we are unbreakable guerreras.

To my sisters, you are my east, north, west, and south. I would be lost without you.

To my daughters, my life, everything I do is for you.

To my *älskling* husband, thank you for your steady love that roots me so strongly I can fly.

And finally to my parents, my fiercest angels. Thanks for continuing to guide me. *Los amaré por siempre.*

Index

addiction. *See* alcohol;
  substance abuse
air, 30–31
alcohol: author's decision to quit
  drinking, 174–175; author's
  experience with, 3, 18, 34,
  69, 165–166, 171–174;
  family history and, 70
altars: author's, 38, 62;
  changing directions and,
  62; as gift, 216; inviting
  ancestors to, 62; limpias for,
  62; Rita on, 98–99
alumbre, 39
ancestors: closeness of, 64–65,
  71–72; connecting with,
  70; inviting to altar, 62;
  letters to, 61, 74, 76;
  pregnancy and, 63–64;
  researching, 67–68
anger, 52–53, 55–56, 102
anxiety, 54
atole, 81
Avila, Elena, 17, 88, 140

bilis, 55, 56
BIPOC, 136, 143, 161

body: childbirth and, 154–155;
  dancing and, 145, 151–152,
  155, 159; feeling alive and,
  158–159; four paths to
  rootedness and, 160–162;
  hiking and, 145–149,
  153–154, 155, 157, 161–162;
  as messenger, 170–171;
  sickness and, 156–157; yoga
  practice, 155–156

capirotada, 88–89
caretaking role, 11, 53
Catholic church, 114
ceiba tree, 194
Chavez, Cesar, 67
chileatole recipe (Lupe's), 92
cleaning, 31, 39, 178, 181
colonization: botanical
  knowledge and, 114–115;
  effects of, 49–50; finding
  your 52 percent and,
  143–144; generational
  trauma and, 18; parenting
  and, 209; self-doubt and,
  198
community, 25, 27, 161–162